Table of Contents

Teacher Introduction

The sixth grade student has already learned a great deal about the library and the wealth of materials that can be found there. *Complete Library Skills* for grade 6 provides a good review of the Dewey Decimal Classification®, the card catalog, magazines, encyclopedias, and indices.

We live in an information age. The world is becoming smaller as we are able to send and receive information faster. That is why computers have become an important part of our world. They enable information to be sent quickly and easily anywhere at any time. This ability to find and receive information via the computer by searching electronic library card catalogs in your school or around the world is truly amazing. This book includes tips for using the electronic card catalog, as well as sample printouts and worksheets on using the printouts for actual research. Also included is information on how to search the Internet, focusing on the World Wide Web. There are worksheets for using good keywords and for evaluating Web sites. You will, of course, know your own and your students' knowledge of computers best. Most of the pages in this book do not actually require the use of a computer, though some do. Check with your librarian if you are unsure what computerized resources your library has. Use the student activities in this book as they appear or modify them to suit your class.

The main focus of *Complete Library Skills* for grade 6 is research. Sixth grade is a time when elementary students have transitioned to middle school or are preparing to switch to a junior high. This is a wonderful time to help these students learn how to use the library and its reference materials for writing research reports. In this book, students will learn how to choose a topic, formulate a research question, prepare for research, use print and electronic research materials, read and create graphic organizers, take notes, compile a report, and cite both print and electronic sources.

Most important to a study of library skills is that students learn to use their skills in practical situations. With that in mind, modify the activities in this book to suit your classroom experiences, your school library, and your community library. The world of electronic technology is opening up vast new opportunities for learning, gathering, and sharing information. Use these tools to help your students become life-long learners.

Complete Library Skills

Grade 6

Published by Instructional Fair
an imprint of
Frank Schaffer Publications®

Author: Linda Turrell
Editor: Cary Malaski

Frank Schaffer Publications®

Instructional Fair is an imprint of Frank Schaffer Publications.

Send all inquiries to:
Frank Schaffer Publications
8720 Orion Place
Columbus, Ohio 43240-2111

Complete Library Skills—grade 6

ISBN 0-7424-1956-8

3 4 5 6 7 8 9 10 MAZ 11 10 09 08 07

Name _____ Date _____

What's in the Library?

By the time you reach sixth grade, you've been in the library enough times to know the basics—a library is full of books. But do you know some of the other useful things that might be hiding someplace in your library?

▶ **Look at the list below. Match each item to its correct description. Then choose two resources and describe how you might use each one.**

Resource

1. _____ atlas

2. _____ librarian

3. _____ shelf labels

4. _____ browser station

5. _____ information posters

6. _____ geographical dictionary

7. _____ CD-ROMs

8. _____ globe

9. _____ almanac

10. _____ thesaurus

Description

a. disks with searchable databases or games

b. yearly publication with statistics on various events

c. spherical map of the world

d. a book of words and their synonyms

e. a bound collection of maps

f. a professional guide to the library

g. identifies what is located on a shelf

h. collection of computers that search the library catalog

i. colorful pictures with useful facts on them

j. information, including spellings of places in the world

▶ **Now describe how you would use the resources.**

11. _____

_____

_____

12. _____

_____

_____

Using the System

The Dewey Decimal Classification® is a system that uses the Dewey number and the first two letters of the author's last name. The books are then arranged in number order first and alphabetical order second.

Here is a list to help you review the ten sections of the library.

000–099 **General Reference**
Atlas, Dictionary, Encyclopedia

100–199 **Philosophy & Psychology**
Ideas of Humankind

200–299 **Religion**

300–399 **Social Science**
Fairy Tales, Fables, Government, Laws

400–499 **Language**

500–599 **Science**
Rocks, Animals, Insects

600–699 **Useful Arts**
Cooking, Pet Care, Farming

700–799 **Fine Arts**
Sports, Arts & Crafts, Photography

800–899 **Literature**
Poems, Plays, Short Stories, Novels

900–999 **History**
Geography, Travel, Biography, History

The 100 Divisions

The following is a closer look at the ten Dewey Decimal Classification® divisions.

000 Generalities
010 Bibliography
020 Library & information sciences
030 General encyclopedic works
040 (not used)
050 General serial publications
060 General organizations & museology
070 Journalism, publishing, newspapers
080 General collections
090 Manuscripts & book rarities

100 Philosophy
110 Metaphysics
120 Epistemology, causation, humankind
130 Paranormal phenomena & arts
140 Specific philosophical viewpoints
150 Psychology
160 Logic
170 Ethics (Moral philosophy)
180 Ancient, Medieval, Oriental
190 Modern western philosophy

200 Religion
210 Natural religion
220 Bible
230 Christian theology
240 Christian moral & devotional
250 Local church & religious orders
260 Social & ecclesiastical theology
270 History & geography of church
280 Christian denominations & sects
290 Other & comparative religions

300 Social Sciences
310 Statistics
320 Political science
330 Economics
340 Law
350 Public administration
360 Social problems & services
370 Education
380 Commerce (Trade)
390 Customs, etiquette, folklore

400 Language
410 Linguistics
420 English & Anglo-Saxon languages
430 Germanic languages, German
440 Romance Languages, French
450 Italian, Romanian, Rhaeto-Romantic
460 Spanish & Portuguese languages
470 Italic languages, Latin
480 Hellenic, Classical Greek
490 Other languages

500 Pure Sciences
510 Mathematics
520 Astronomy & allied sciences
530 Physics
540 Chemistry & allied sciences
550 Science of Earth & other worlds
560 Paleontology, Paleozoology
570 Life sciences
580 Botanical sciences
590 Zoological sciences

600 Technology (Applied Sciences)
610 Medical sciences, medicine
620 Engineering & allied operations
630 Agriculture & related technologies
640 Home economics & family living

650 Management & auxiliary services
660 Chemical & related technologies
670 Manufacturers
680 Manufacture for specific uses
690 Buildings

700 The Arts
710 Civic & landscape art
720 Architecture
730 Plastic arts & sculpture
740 Drawing, decorative & minor arts
750 Painting & paintings
760 Graphic arts & prints
770 Photography & photographs
780 Music
790 Recreational & performing arts

800 Literature
810 American literature in English
820 English & Anglo-Saxon literatures
830 Literature of Germanic languages
840 Literature of Romance languages
850 Italian, Romanian, Rhaeto-Romantic
860 Spanish & Portuguese literature
870 Italic literatures, Latin
880 Hellenic literatures, Greek
890 Literatures of other languages

900 Geography and History
910 General geography & travel
920 General biography & genealogy
930 General history of ancient world
940 General history of Europe
950 General history of Asia
960 General history of Africa
970 General history of North America
980 General history of South America
990 General history of other areas

Understanding the Decimal in the System

You have probably noticed that the class numbers of some books contain decimals. You have learned that there are ten main classes in the Dewey Decimal Classification®. You have also learned that each of the ten main classes is composed of ten divisions. Let's use the 700s, The Arts, as an example. One of the divisions of the 700s is 790—Recreational and Performing Arts. The 790s may be divided into ten sections, as follows.

790	Recreational and performing arts	795	Games of chance
791	Public performances	796	Athletic and outdoor sports and games
792	Theater (Stage presentations)	797	Aquatic and air sports
793	Indoor games and amusements	798	Equestrian sports and animal racing
794	Indoor games of skill	799	Fishing, hunting, shooting

Each of the above sections may be expanded as far as necessary by using numbers after a decimal point. The 796 section could be broken up like this:

796	Athletic and outdoor sports and games	796.33	Inflated ball driven by foot
796.1	Miscellaneous games	796.332	American football
796.2	Active games requiring equipment	796.334	Soccer
796.3	Ball games	796.34	Racket games
796.31	Ball thrown or hit by hand	796.342	Tennis (lawn tennis)
796.32	Inflated ball thrown or hit by hand	796.35	Ball driven by club, mallet, bat
		796.352	Golf
		796.357	Baseball

▶ **Where would you find...**

handball? _____

volleyball? _____

It's Got Class

Decide in which of the ten main classes each of the following nonfiction books would be found. Write both the number and the name of the class.

1. *Compton's Encyclopedia* _____

2. *Thanksgiving* _____

3. *Best-Loved Folktales of the World* _____

4. *Putting on a Play* _____

5. *Abe Lincoln Grows Up* _____

6. *Paul Bunyan Swings His Axe* _____

7. *Bible Stories for Children* _____

8. *Webster's New Student Dictionary* _____

9. *Space Shuttle* _____

10. *The American Revolution* _____

11. *The Land and People of Canada* _____

12. *Easter Chimes, Stories for Easter and the Spring Season* _____

_____

13. *Tigers* _____

14. *Johnny Appleseed and Other Poems* _____

15. *The World of Dance* _____

Name _____ Date _____

Research Situations

Read each situation. What division do you need?

1. You need a book about butterflies. Where do you look?_____

2. You need to make a poster for "safety in sports week." You also plan to win the contest for best poster. Where do you look? _____

3. Your school plans a celebration to mark its twenty-fifth anniversary. Where do you find a picture of the sycamore leaf (your school emblem)?_____

4. Your cousin plans a visit. He knows everything about soccer. Where do you go to read up on the subject? _____

5. Where can you find information about the American colonies?_____

6. You are starting a new hobby—painting. Where do you look? _____

7. Where can you find information about famous sports stars?_____

8. Where can you find help in training your new puppy? _____

9. Where can you find help in setting up your new aquarium?_____

10. Where can you find information about black holes in space? _____

What Subject Division?

Read each title or subject below. In what division would you find it? You may check the charts from pages 6 and 7 if you need help.

Subjects

1. rocks _____

2. stars _____

3. sea animals _____

4. coral _____

5. whales _____

6. cooking _____

7. sports _____

8. history _____

9. drawing _____

10. biography _____

Titles

11. *Learning French* _____

12. *Making Costumes* _____

13. *The Pioneers* _____

14. *Life in the American Colonies* _____

15. *Whales and Other Sea Animals* _____

16. *The Romans* _____

17. *Soccer!* _____

18. *Learning Spanish* _____

19. *Sports in America* _____

20. *Explorers in America* _____

What Division Do You Need?

➤ **Read each situation. Choose a division. Write the number and the subject.**

1. You need a book about sports. You aren't certain if you will join the soccer or baseball team. _____ _____

2. You need a book about the lives of famous people. You need to write about a famous person for your report. _____ _____

3. You are interested in the traditions and customs of Ireland.

_____ _____

4. You are looking for a fairy tale to read to your young cousin.

_____ _____

5. You need a book that will teach you Spanish so that you can talk to the new student in class. _____ _____

6. You need a book about baking cookies. You volunteered to bake a batch for a school party. _____ _____

7. You are doing a report about American colonies.

_____ _____

8. Your parents plan to travel to Maine. You are going too, but you need to know what type of clothes to wear. _____ _____

9. Your new neighbors are Hindu. But you know nothing about this religion. Where can you find more information? _____ _____

10. Your assignment is to compare whales and sharks. Where can you find more information? _____ _____

Putting Call Numbers in Order

▶ **Put the following call numbers in the order in which you would find them on the shelves in a library. Remember, if two books have the same class number they will be arranged by the author's last name. Write the numbers 1–5 on the lines to put the call numbers in order.**

1. _____ 977.6 Fi

_____ 976.4 Be

_____ 977 Al

_____ 973.7 Ki

_____ 977.6 Wh

4. _____ 629.1309 Re

_____ 629.109 Le

_____ 629.13 Ze

_____ 629.2 Ta

_____ 629.14 Po

2. _____ 301.45 Me

_____ 301.45 Ab

_____ 301.42 Ja

_____ 301.24 Ba

_____ 301.43 Lo

5. _____ 358.007 Ei

_____ 358 Li

_____ 358.407 Er

_____ 358.4 Ll

_____ 358.417 Ca

3. _____ 537.2 Bi

_____ 537 Si

_____ 537.5 Lo

_____ 537.2 Fl

_____ 538 Ti

6. _____ 330.973 Fi

_____ 330.9798 Hu

_____ 330.942 Sm

_____ 331.88 Fo

_____ 331.86 Kl

Name _____   Date _____

Using the Card Catalog

The card catalog is divided into three sections. You can find a card for every book in your library under a title, a subject, or an author. This is the information you can find on a card:

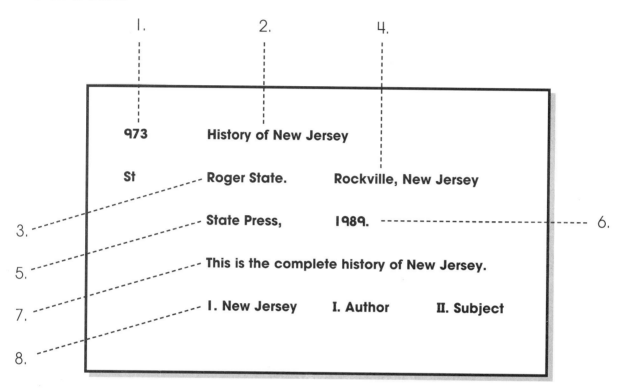

```
            1.              2.              4.


     973           History of New Jersey

     St            Roger State.      Rockville, New Jersey

3.                 State Press,      1989.                          6.

5.                 This is the complete history of New Jersey.

7.                 I. New Jersey      I. Author      II. Subject

8.
```

1. Call number
2. Book title
3. Author
4. Place of publication
5. Publisher
6. Copyright date
7. Summary of the book
8. Tracing—other places in the card catalog where you can find this book

1. What other catalog cards would you look for to find this book? _____

_____

Comparing Cards

➡ **Use the cards below to answer the questions.**

```
              The Planets

   Z     Solar, Jason.

   567            Planets/

   So    Jason Solar—Startown, N.Y.: Galaxy Press, 1999.

              xiv, 323 p.; 25 cm.—(Tells about the planets in the solar system)

          I. Planets      I. Author      II. Subject.
```

```
          Stars, Galaxies, and the Planets

   Z     System, Peter.

   567         Stars, Galaxies, and the Planets/

   Sy    Peter System—Milky Way Town, N.Y.: Milky Way Press, 1997.

              xiv, 118 p.;18 cm.—(Tells about stars, galaxies, and planets)

          I. Planets       I. Author      II. Subject
```

1. _____ What are the call numbers?

2. _____ Which book is the newest?

3. _____ Name the publisher of each book.

4. _____ What is the call number of *The Planets?*

5. _____ What book was published in Milky Way Town, NY?

6. _____ Under which subject will you find these books?

7. _____ Who is the author of *The Planets?*

8. _____ Who is the author of *Stars, Galaxies, and the Planets?*

9. _____ Where was *The Planets* published?

10. _____ In which state were both books published?

Name _____ Date _____

What Card Catalog Do You Need?

▶ **Read each research situation. Decide which card will help you and then write** *author,* *title,* **or** *subject* **on the line.**

1. _____ Did Roger Peterson write a mystery book called *Green Tree*?

2. _____ Are there any books about hamsters?

3. _____ Are there any books about rocks and minerals?

4. _____ Are there any books about boats?

5. _____ Did Peter Johnson write a book called *Over the Mountain*?

6. _____ Are there enough books about ants in the library for all 23 students to check one out?

7. _____ Did Roger Ant write *All About Ants*?

8. _____ Are there any books about space in your library?

9. _____ Is *Green Fire* in your library?

10. _____ Did John James write a fairy tale called *Peter Bunkins*?

Name That Card

Read each problem. Write whether you need an *author*, *subject*, or *title* card on the line.

1. _____ *History of Toys*

2. _____ toys

3. _____ Alfred B. Toy

4. _____ *Cooking for Kids*

5. _____ Alfred B. Cook

6. _____ cooking

7. _____ *Native Americans of the West*

8. _____ Arthur C. Chippewa

9. _____ Native Americans

10. _____ *Goldfish and Other Pets*

11. _____ rocks and minerals

12. _____ *Stories for Young*

13. _____ Jerome C. Johnson

14. _____ *How to Raise Your Gerbil*

15. _____ gerbils

The Electronic Catalog

Libraries use a special organizing system. Most often this organizing system is in the form of a library catalog on a computer. You use the browser station at your library to search the catalog for a particular item. There are several ways to find a book from the browser station. You can search by:

- title
- subject
- author
- keyword

Search Tips

- Remember that when you search you should not include the words *a, an,* or *the.*

- Pay special attention to how your browser asks for information. For example, it may want the *last name* of an author first, then the *first name.*

- Be as specific as you can to narrow your search.

▶ **Use the browser station to search for the following in your school library catalog. Then answer the questions.**

1. Do an author search for Richard Peck. How many titles come up? _____

2. Do a keyword or subject search for *pig.* How many titles come up? _____

3. Do a title search for *The Day No Pigs Would Die.* How many titles come up?

   _____

4. Based on the questions above, what have you learned about using technology to search? _____

   _____

   _____

   _____

Name _____ Date _____

Author Search

You go to your library's browser station and search for the author Brett Fastlane. You type in *Brett Fastlane* and don't get any records. The browser asks for the last name first, so you type *Fastlane, Brett*. Several books come up, but you select the one you are most interested in—*Safety Practices in Professional Racing.*

► **Here is the record that comes up on your computer screen. Use it to answer the questions that follow.**

Author	Fastlane, Brett
Title	Safety Practices in Professional Racing
Pub Info	Indiana: 500 Press, c2002
Description	96 p. photo.
Location (call #)	796.72 Fas
Summary	This book reviews some of the worst accidents in NASCAR racing history and the effects on racing practices.
Subject	Car racing

1. What year was the book published? _____

2. What is the call number? _____

3. How many pages are in the book? _____

4. Who is the publisher of the book? Where is that publisher located? _____
   _____

5. If you were doing a report about types of racecars, would this book be useful?
   Explain. _____
   _____
   _____
   _____

Title Search

A title search is the most specific of all the searches. There are a few tricks, however. Rob heard about a book about a hockey player that he would like to read. He thinks the title is *The Captain,* so he types in the following in the title search.

Title Search   the captain

1. What did Rob do that was unnecessary? Explain. _____

   _____

2. Does it matter whether you use capital letters when searching? Try it! _____

   _____

▶ **Here are the results of Rob's search. Use it to answer the questions that follow.**

Number	Title	Year
1	The Captain (audio recording)	2001
	Books on Tape	
2	The Captain / Justin Michael	2000
3	The Captain / Oliver Townsend	1945

3. Rob is sure that the book he wants was recently published. Which record should

   he choose? Explain. _____

   _____

4. What should Rob expect to find if he looks for record number 1 on the library

   shelves? _____

Name _____ Date _____

Subject Search

Even though you think they are fun to watch, your dad is going nuts trying to keep the squirrels away from the bird feeder. During your library time, you decide to find a book to help him. You aren't sure where to start, so you do a subject search for "squirrels."

▶ **Here is what comes up on your computer screen. Use it to answer the questions.**

Number	Subjects (1–5 of 5)	Entries Found
1	Squirrels	11
2	Squirrel Control	4
3	Squirrel Humor	3
4	Squirrel Fiction Literature	8
5	Squirrel Sound Recordings	1

1. Which of the subjects above best narrows your search? _____

2. Which other subject might have helpful information? _____

▶ **After making your selection, another screen comes up. Use it to answer the question that follows.**

Subject

Squirrel Control

Number	Title (1–2 of 2)	Year
1	Outwitting Squirrels	2001
2	Techniques for Trapping Squirrels	1987

3. Which of the above titles would you choose to help your dad? Explain. _____

_____

_____

Keyword Search

Carlos loves to play soccer. He wants to find some soccer books to bring home from his school library. He knows that he should type in the word *soccer,* but doesn't know which would be better— a keyword search or a subject search. He decides to try both.

A keyword search returns over 200 records—too many! A subject search returns 75 records—still too many. Since he's not sure of the exact subject he's interested in, he goes back to the keyword search. This time he uses a suggestion on the screen and types *soccer AND training.* Aha! This time a list of 8 titles comes up, and they are just what he's looking for.

▶ **Answer the questions based on Carlos's experience with searches.**

1. Which appears to be more accurate, a subject search or a keyword search?

   _____

2. Why did adding the word *AND* help Carlos's search?

   _____

3. What do you think would have happened if Carlos had typed in *soccer NOT training?* _____

4. A keyword search looks over the entire record for a word, but a subject search only looks in the subject headings for the word. When might a keyword search be more helpful? When might a subject search be more helpful? Explain.

   _____

   _____

   _____

Name _____ Date _____

How to Read the Online Card Catalog

When you check out the card catalog in your library, you go to one location. Sometimes you may need to wait if someone else is using the drawer that you need. But if your library has an automated system, there might be more than one computer station or terminal set up to access the catalog. Since the access time can be fairly quick, you may not have to wait very long to get the information you need.

If the library's computer terminal is already turned on, you will probably see a main menu with a list of items to choose from to begin your search. Among the main menu items will be the computerized card catalog of books and other library holdings. Other holdings could include videos, compact discs, read-a-longs, filmstrips, slides, microforms, cassettes, art prints, scores, and maps. Also listed will be a newspaper and magazine index. Sometimes this index contains actual complete articles. If so, this can save you time by allowing you to scan an article to determine its usefulness. Access to the Internet, as well as to other electronically connected libraries and their holdings, may also be listed in the main menu. These items may appear with headings such as *Internet,* the letters WWW (for World Wide Web), or by using the suffix *–net,* as in COUNTYNET

 Look at the results of a catalog search below. Answer the question.

Call Number	Author	Title	Publisher	© Date
641.3 Hyd	Hyde, Margaret O.	What Have You Been Eating? Do You Really Know?	McGraw,	1975

1. In what section and division of the library is the book located?_____

_____

How to Read the Online Card Catalog (cont.)

Another form that systems might use to present information would look something like the following.

Author:	Hull, Gloria T.
Title:	Healing Heart: poems, 1973–1988
Publisher:	Kitchen Table: Women of Color Press, ©1989.
Subjects:	Afro-American women poets.
	American poetry-20th century.
Library Holdings:	
Call Number:	811.54 Hul – Paperback – Available

In most OPACs, you will be given the option to see more information about the book you've selected. Follow the directions or commands shown on the computer screen to get this detailed information or to start a new or revised search.

▶ **Use the search result above to answer the questions.**

2. In what section and division of the library is this book located?_____

_____

3. Can you check this book out?_____

4. If you wanted more books by this author, how would you search for them?

_____

_____

_____

Let's Get Cooking: Reading an OPAC

▶ **A subject search on *cooking* was conducted, and the results are shown in the sample printout of available library books found on page 27. Read the printout to review the author, book title, and other information listed. Using that information, answer the following questions. Write your answers on the lines provided.**

1. Is there a book about microwave cooking? _____
   If so, what is its title? _____

2. What book titles are available on African cooking? _____

3. What book titles deal with Japanese cooking? _____

4. Can you find a book about vegetarian cooking? _____
   What is its title? _____

5. What is the complete bibliographic information on a book that deals with low-fat cooking? _____
   _____

6. How many books were written by Dale Brown? _____

7. What company publishes Dale Brown's books? _____

8. What cookbooks would provide recipes for those watching their weight?
   _____
   _____

Let's Get Cooking: Reading an OPAC (cont.)

Use the sample OPAC printout of library books on the subject of *cooking* on page 27 to answer the following questions. Write your answers on the lines provided.

1. What are the copyright dates of Dale Brown's books? _____

2. Who is the author of *Cooking from the Gourmet's Garden*? _____

3. What books could you use to find recipes for Indian food? _____
   _____

4. What is the copyright date of the book written by Mary Jane Finsand? _____

5. What countries or regional areas has Jules Bond written about? _____
   _____

6. Who are the publishers of Jules Bond's books, and when were his books
   published? _____
   _____
   _____

7. Who wrote a book on Mexican cooking? _____

8. Are the publishers listed in every entry? _____

9. What books would provide recipes for Italian and Scandinavian food?
   _____
   _____

Name _____ Date _____

Let's Get Cooking: Reading an OPAC (cont.)

Call Number	Author	Title	Publisher	Date
641.5 BRO	Brown, Dale.	American Cooking.	Time-Life,	1968.
641.5 BRO	Brown, Dale.	American Cooking: The Northwest.	Time-Life,	1970.
641.5 FIN	Finsand, Mary Jane.	The Complete Diabetic Cookbook.	Sterling,	1990.
641.5 WOL	Wolfe, Robert L. and Diane Wolfe.	Vegetarian Cooking Around the World.	Lerner Publications,	1992.
641.5 BON	Bond, Jules J.	The Chinese Cuisine I Love.	Ameil,	1977.
641.5 BON	Bond, Jules J.	The French Cuisine I Love.	Ameil,	1977.
641.5 BON	Bond, Jules J.	The Mid-Eastern Cuisine I Love.	Ameil,	1977.
641.5 BON	Bond, Jules J.	Recipes from Around the World.	Barron's,	1984.
641.5 CAS	Castle, Coralie.	Cooking from the Gourmet's Garden.	Cole Group,	1994.
641.5 LIN	Linsay, Rae.	The International Party Cookbook.	Drake,	1972.
641.5 LON	Longstreet, Stephen.	The Joys of Jewish Cooking.	Weathervane,	1988. ©1974.
641.4 MAW	Mawson, Monica.	Cooking With Herbs and Spices.	Domus,	1978.
641.5 GAS	Gaspari, Claudia.	Food in Italy.	Rourke Publications,	1989.
641.5 GOM	Gomez, Paolo.	Food in Mexico.	Rourke Publications,	1989.
641.5 NID	Nidetch, Jean.	Watching Your Weight Cookbook.	New American,	1978.
641.5 OJA	Ojakangas, Beatrice.	Scandinavian Cooking.	H. P. Books,	1983.
641.5 TSU	Tsuji, Shizuo.	Japanese Cooking.	Kodansha International,	1980.
641.5 VAN	Van Der Post, L.	African Cooking.	Time-Life,	1970.
641.5 KAU	Kaur, Sharon.	Food in India.	Rourke Publications,	1989.
641.5 DOE	Doeser, Linda.	Complete Microwave Cookbook.	International Culinary Society,	1990. ©1989.
641.5 KER	Kerr, Graham.	A Low Fat, Heart Healthy Cookbook.	G. P. Putnam's,	1995.

Audio Equipment: Reading an OPAC II

▶ **Read the computer printout on pages 30-31 for *Audio Equipment—Automobiles*. Write the name of the article and the magazine that it is found in for each of the following research questions. Use the lines provided for your answers.**

1. Where can you find information about car stereo basics? _____

_____

2. What stereo system is available in a Ford Mustang? _____

_____

3. Where can you find suggestions for the best sounding systems? _____

_____

4. What stereo is best for your type of car? _____

_____

5. Where can you get information on the history of the audio system in the Ford Mustang? _____

_____

6. What journals contain articles on aftermarket car stereos? _____

_____

Name _____ Date _____

Audio Equipment: Reading an OPAC II (cont.)

➡ Read the computer printout on pages 30-31 for *Audio Equipment—Automobiles*. Identify the articles to use to research the following questions. Write your answers on the lines below.

1. How can you reduce the possibility of audio system theft? _____
_____
_____

2. What do the stereo systems of the Ford Mustang and Dodge Intrepid have in common? _____
_____

3. How can you upgrade your stereo system? _____
_____

4. How can you make your car appear as if it has no stereo? _____
_____

5. Where can you see photographs of car stereos? _____
_____

6. Where can you find information on the Lexus GS300's audio system? _____
_____

7. Where can you get information on car stereo speakers? _____
_____

Audio Equipment—Automobiles

Record 1

Access No:	01898914	ProQuest Resource/One
Title:	Car stereo update	
Author:	Pohlmann, Ken C.	
Journal:	Home Mechanix (GHMX)	ISSN: 8755-0423
	Jrnl Group: Lifestyles	Vol: 90 Iss: 784
	Date: Apr 1994	p: 84–88
	Type: Feature	Length: Long
	Illus: Illustration; Photograph	
Subjects:	Audio equipment; Loudspeakers; Automobiles	
Abstracts:	Aftermarket car audio equipment has been popular since the 1970s, but car manufacturers are now offering systems that rival the aftermarket's best. The basics of car stereos and which ones are better for certain types of cars are discussed.	
Item Availability:	CD-ROM	

Record 2

Access No:	01556532	ProQuest Resource/One
Title:	Stealth stereo upgrades	
Author:	Berger, Ivan	
Journal:	Home Mechanix (GHMX)	ISSN: 8755-0423
	Jrnl Group: Lifestyles	Vol: 89 Iss: 776
	Date: Jun 1993	p: 42–44
	Type: Feature	Length: Medium
	Illus: Photograph	
Subjects:	Automobile; Theft; Radio equipment; Audio equipment	
Abstract:	Automobile owners can reduce the risk of theft when upgrading a car's sound system by making it appear factory-stock.	

Audio Equipment: Reading an OPAC II (cont.)

Audio Equipment—Automobiles

Record 3

Access No:	01922961	ProQuest Resource/One
Title:	Road music	
Author:	Vizard, Frank	
Journal:	Popular Mechanics (GPOM)	ISSN: 0032-4558
	Jrnl Group: Lifestyles; Sci/Tech	Vol: 170 Iss: 11
	Date: Nov 1993	p: 128–129
	Type: Feature	Length: Medium
	Illus: Illustration; Photograph	
Subjects:	Audio equipment; Automobiles	

Abstract: Many new cars, including the Ford Mustang, Lexus GS300, and Dodge Intrepid, feature impressive audio systems. The audio systems of the three cars are examined.

Item Availability: CD-ROM

Record 4

Access No:	01874610	ProQuest Resource/One
Title:	Signals: Pony car	
Author:	Pohlman, Ken C.	
Journal:	Stereo Review (GSTR)	ISSN: 0039-1220
	Jrnl Group: Lifestyles	Vol: 59 Iss: 3
	Date: Mar 1994	p: 25
	Type: Commentary	Length: Short
	Illus: Illustration	
Subjects:	Automobiles; Audio equipment; Design	

Abstract: In 1994, the Ford Mustang is celebrating its thirtieth birthday with a complete redesign. The car's audio system shows just how far car audio has come over the years.

Item Availability: CD-ROM

Genres of Literature

Match each genre with its definition by writing a number on each book.

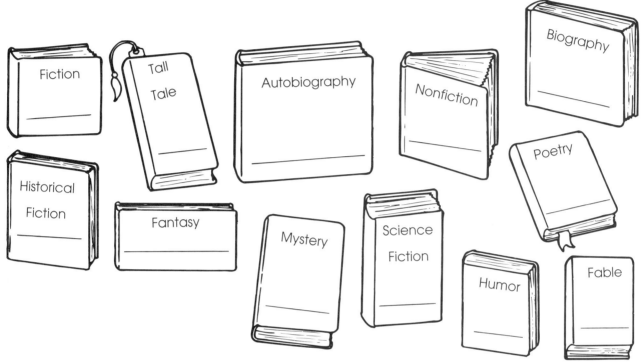

1. a story about a puzzling crime

2. a true story

3. a true story about a person's life written by someone other than that person

4. a story so exaggerated it could not be true

5. a true story of a person's life written by that person

6. a make-believe (not true) story

7. a verse or rhyme

8. a story about future events and future technology

9. a funny story

10. a make-believe story about a real person or a real time that existed in the past

11. a brief story that teaches a moral—often containing animal characters

12. a story about unusual characters and make-believe places

Can You Tell a Book by Its Cover?

Match each book title with its genre or description by writing the correct letter on the blank.

1. _____ *Cousin Clara's Creative Cuisine*

2. _____ *The Case of the Ancient Aardvark*

3. _____ *Love Me Tender*

4. _____ *How the Nose Got Its Sniffles*

5. _____ *Time to Rhyme (or Not)*

6. _____ *A Volume of Verbosity*

7. _____ *Where Am I?*

8. _____ *Mama's Walk to Kyoto*

9. _____ *Mein Hund Ist Gesund*

10. _____ *Music to My Ears*

11. _____ *Where Are the Clones?*

12. _____ *Brandin', Punchin', Eatin' Dust*

13. _____ *Like a Diamond*

14. _____ *Hey, Diddle!*

15. _____ *Tut Tut, Tut!*

16. _____ *A Knight to Remember*

17. _____ *Eureka! It's a Hoover!*

18. _____ *Give 'er Some Gas!*

19. _____ *Faces for Wheaties*

20. _____ *Easel Down the Road*

21. _____ *In Other Words*

22. _____ *Compost Is Your Friend*

23. _____ *If You Could Read My Mind*

24. _____ *Shake, Rattle, and Roll*

25. _____ *I Am What I Am*

a. atlas

b. myth

c. gardening

d. engine repair

e. song book

f. romance

g. autobiography

h. sports stars

i. East Asian folk tale

j. cooking

k. American dance

l. inventions

m. nursery rhymes

n. science fiction

o. mystery

p. poetry

q. thesaurus

r. medieval history

s. American history

t. ESP

u. dictionary

v. foreign language

w. art appreciation

x. stars

y. Ancient Egypt

Newbery and Caldecott Award Winners

The following lists highlight the last 15 years of Newbery and Caldecott award winners.

Newbery Award Winners

2003: *Crispin: The Cross of Lead* by Avi

2002: *A Single Shard* by Linda Sue Park

2001: *A Year Down Yonder* by Richard Peck

2000: *Bud, Not Buddy* by Christopher Paul Curtis

1999: *Holes* by Louis Sachar

1998: *Out of the Dust* by Karen Hesse

1997: *The View from Saturday* by E. L. Konigsburg

1996: *The Midwife's Apprentice* by Karen Cushman

1995: *Walk Two Moons* by Sharon Creech

1994: *The Giver* by Lois Lowry

1993: *Missing May* by Cynthia Rylant

1992: *Shiloh* by Phyllis Reynolds Naylor

1991: *Maniac Magee* by Jerry Spinelli

1990: *Number the Stars* by Lois Lowry

1989: *Joyful Noise: Poems for Two Voices* by Paul Fleischman

Caldecott Award Winners

2003: *My Friend Rabbit* by Eric Rohmann

2002: *The Three Pigs* by David Wiesner

2001: *So You Want to Be President?* by David Small

2000: *Joseph Had a Little Overcoat* by Simms Taback

1999: *Snowflake Bentley* by Mary Azarian

1998: *Rapunzel* by Paul O. Zelinsky

1997: *Golem* by David Wisniewski

1996: *Officer Buckle and Gloria* by Peggy Rathmann

1995: *Smoky Night* by David Diaz

1994: *Grandfather's Journey* by Allen Say

1993: *Mirette on the High Wire* by Emily Arnold McCully

1992: *Tuesday* by David Wiesner

1991: *Black and White* by David Macaulay

1990: *Lon Po Po: A Red-Riding Hood Story from China* by Ed Young

1989: *Song and Dance Man* by Stephen Gammell

Suggested Books for Sixth Grade Readers

Nonfiction

Eleanor Roosevelt: A Life of Discovery
  by Russell Freedman

Moon and I by Betsy Byars

Puppies, Dogs and Blue Northers
  by Gary Paulsen

Fiction

6th Grade Can Really Kill You
  by Barthe DeClements

The 6th Grade Nickname Game
  by Gordon Korman

Anastasia's Chosen Career
  by Lois Lowry

The Barn by Avi

The Boggart by Susan Cooper

Bull Run by Paul Fleischman

Chasing Redbird by Sharon Creech

Everywhere by Bruce Brooks

A Family Apart by Joan Lowery Nixon

The Firebug Connection
  by Jean Craighead George

The Ghost in the Mirror
  by John Bellairs

Hatchet by Gary Paulsen

Holes by Louis Sacher

Journey Home by Yoshiko Uchida

Lyddie by Katherine Paterson

The Merlin Effect by T. A. Barron

Our Sixth Grade Sugar Babies
  by Eve Bunting

Park's Quest by Katherine Paterson

Secret Garden
  by Frances Hodgson Burnett

Sixth Grade Secrets by Louis Sachar

Song of the Gargoyle
  by Zilpha Keatley Snyder

Space Brat by Bruce Coville

Stealing Thunder by Mary Casanova

Stowaway by Karen Hesse

Time for Andrew
  by Mary Downing Hahn

Tuck Everlasting by Natalie Babbitt

The Vandemark Mummy
  by Cynthia Voight

The View from Saturday
  by E. L. Konigsburg

The Wanderer by Sharon Creech

The Watsons Go to Birmingham
  by Christopher Paul Curtis

The Westing Game by Ellen Raskin

What Could Go Wrong
  by Willo Davis Roberts

Wintering by William Durbin

The Wonderful Wizard of Oz
  by L. Frank Baum

Wrapped in Riddle by Sharon Heisel

Zach's Lie by Roland Smith

Suggested Authors for Sixth Grade Readers

Entries are written with author's last name first and include a featured book by each author.

Avi	*(Nothing But the Truth)*
Babbitt, Natalie	*(Tuck Everlasting)*
Barron, T. A.	*(Heartlight)*
Bauer, Marion	*(On My Honor)*
Brooks, Bruce	*(The Moves Make the Man)*
Byars, Betsy	*(The Pinballs)*
Curtis, Christopher Paul	*(Bud, Not Buddy)*
Cormier, Robert	*(I Am the Cheese)*
Cushman, Karen	*(Midwife's Apprentice)*
Fleischman, Paul	*(The Borning Room)*
Fox, Paula	*(Monkey Island)*
George, Jean Craighead	*(Julie of the Wolves)*
Hahn, Mary Downing	*(Stepping on the Cracks)*
Jacques, Brian	*(Redwall)*
Lasky, Kathryn	*(The Night Journey)*
Lowry, Lois	*(The Giver)*
Paterson, Katherine	*(Jacob Have I Loved)*
Paulsen, Gary	*(The Foxman)*
Peck, Richard	*(Long Way from Chicago)*
Philbrick, Rodman	*(Freak the Mighty)*
Spinelli, Jerry	*(Maniac Magee)*
Voight, Cynthia	*(Homecoming)*

Internet Searches

A wealth of information is just a click away. You already know this if you've used the Internet. Searching on the Internet is similar to searching your library's catalog, but the results can include most anything that is out there on the Web. When you search the World Wide Web, you use a search engine that looks for sites that match your keywords. Your school librarian can help you find the best search engine to use.

▶ **See if you can find a Web site to answer each of the questions below. First write the words you would use to search. When you find a good site to answer the question, write the name of the site on the line. If you have access to a printer, print each page as you find it.**

1. You are doing a project on Ancient Rome. You need facts on its government, economy, society, and its impact on current times. Where can you find this information? _____

_____

2. Where can you learn what time it is in Greenwich, England?

_____

_____

3. Where can you find information on the maximum speed of the cheetah?

_____

_____

4. Where can you find rules to play the game of mancala?

_____

_____

Searching the Internet

Ask your librarian to help you find the best search engine to use. Then see if you can find a Web site to answer each of the questions below. Write the name of the site on the line. If you have access to a printer, print each page as you find it.

1. Where can you find information on the culture of the Tlingit tribes of Alaska?

_____

_____

2. What site will tell you more about the great white shark and its habitat?

_____

_____

3. Where can you get information about the ancient Byzantines and their capital city? _____

_____

4. Where can you find an antonym for the word *energized?*

_____

_____

5. Where can you find how many people lived in the United States in 2002?

_____

_____

Name _____ Date _____

Keywords and Search Terms

► **Finding information on Web sites is relatively easy if you use the right keywords. Keywords are words that tell the main idea of what you are looking for. In some cases they may be the main ideas of your research question. Read the research question below for an example.**

Can soil pollution affect water pollution in our environment?

The terms in this question that are keywords are *soil pollution, water pollution,* and *our environment.*

► **Read the next research question. What words in it would be good keywords? Write the keywords on the line provided.**

How does the pollution of our waters affect our environment?

_____

Can any of these keywords be combined to create a searchable term?
A searchable term is even more specific than a keyword. In this example, *pollution* and *water* could become the more usable and narrow search term *water pollution.*

Finding Keywords and Search Terms

Find the keywords to begin computer searches for the research questions below. Then combine keywords to create narrow search terms. Write your answers on the lines provided.

1. *What is the major problem of famous sports stars today?*

   keywords _____

   search terms _____

2. *What do you need to know about packing for a vacation?*

   keywords _____

   search terms _____

3. *What do vitamins have to do with nutrition?*

   keywords _____

   search terms _____

4. *How do newspapers explain the events of history?*

   keywords _____

   search terms _____

5. *What do you need to know about caring for a pet?*

   keywords _____

   search terms _____

6. *How do weather patterns in other parts of the world affect the weather in your area?*

   keywords _____

   search terms _____

Name _____ Date _____

Boolean Searches

Many search engines use Boolean searches. In this kind of search you can combine keywords using several different words. Look at the words below.

or   **and**   **and not**

If you are looking for information on Martin Luther King, Jr. but not information on the holiday named after him, you might put in the following:

Martin Luther King **and not** holiday

If you are looking for information on ecology, specifically water pollution, but not in the United States, you might type the following:

ecology **and** water pollution **and not** U.S.A.

▶ **Write Boolean searches for the following research questions. Use the Boolean terms shown in boldface below.**

1. What are the problems of acid rain and the rain forest?

_____ **or** _____ **and** _____

2. How can you make a pizza at home?

_____ **and** _____ **and not** _____

3. How do you groom a longhaired dog?

_____ **and** _____ **and not** _____

4. Where can you find information on battery-operated portable CD players?

_____ **and** _____ **or** _____

5. What are some of the records set by Olympic athletes in 1996?

_____ **or** _____ **and** _____

6. What are the names of music groups poplar with young people today?

_____ **and** _____ **or** _____

                    0-7424-1956-8 *Complete Library Skills*

Name _____ Date _____

Evaluating Online Sources

Not all Web sites are created equal. How do you know whether the site you are using is a good source to use for information? First you should think about your **purpose** for searching the Web. Are you looking for something fun to do? Are you writing a report for class? It's much more important to use quality sources for a report than it is for something you're doing for fun.

▶ **Study the lists below. They will give you some ideas about what to look for when evaluating Web sites. Use them to answer the questions on page 43.**

Good Sources

- accurate; no typing or factual errors

- easy to read and understand; graphics are clear and add to the content being discussed

- include in-depth information

- not biased; contain objective facts

- revised frequently; up-to-date

- from a reliable source; you've heard of the organization sponsoring the page (a URL ending with *.gov*, *.edu*, or *.org* is also a good sign)

- stable; the pages stick around for a long time and are always there when you go back to them

Questionable Sources

- contain typing errors and errors in fact

- difficult to read; graphics are distracting

- information is not detailed or in-depth

- lots of one person's opinions

- page hasn't been revised in a long time

- you've never heard of the person or source sponsoring the page

- here today, gone tomorrow; page is not there when you look for it a few months later

1. You are trying to find help with converting metric units to customary units. Which of the following Web sites would be the best source? Circle your choice. Explain why you picked it.

   a. www.joesmathpage.com

   b. www.library.org/math

   c. www.icanduemath.com

   _____

2. Look at the two screens below. Based on what you see, which is the more reliable source? Circle the source you would use.

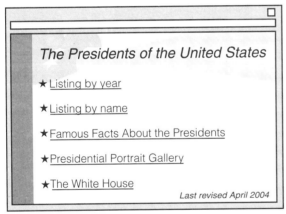

a.

The Presidents of the United States

★ Listing by year

★ Listing by name

★ Famous Facts About the Presidents

★ Presidential Portrait Gallery

★ The White House

Last revised April 2004

b.

All About President of the U.S.

Click here! for a list of all the Presidence

The best president was Abraham Lincoln.

Last revised December 1999

Pictures I drew of the Presidents.

3. Your friend Anthony needs help finding information for a report. He wants to use the World Wide Web, but doesn't even know where to begin. Make a "Best of the Web" list for Anthony of the four most reputable sources you know of to find information. You may ask your teacher or school librarian to help get you started. Write the addresses on the lines below.

   _____

   _____

   _____

   _____

Name _____ Date _____

Can You Spy the Best Site?

Read each of the research situations presented here and on page 45. Determine which of the Web sites listed would be the best source of information. More than one site may sound appealing, but you are to choose the best and most reliable source. (Look back at the chart on page 42 for help with evaluating sources.) Circle the letter of your choice. Then write why you chose that site.

I. You are writing a report about lions and are looking for some facts about lions kept in zoos.

    a. The National Zoo

       http://natzoo.si.edu

    b. Lucy's Lion Lovers Page

       http://www.lucyluvslions.com

    c. National Aquarium

       http://www.aqua.org

_____

_____

2. In social studies, you are learning about the White House. Your class has been divided into groups to make a speech to the class. Your group is to talk about presidential pets that have lived in the White House.

    a. White House Pets

       http://www.homepage.com/jrolfe/pets

    b. Dogs in the White House

       http://mysite.presidentdogs.com

    c. The White House

       http://www.whitehouse.gov/kids/

_____

_____

Can You Spy the Best Site? (cont.)

3. Your science fair project is due in four weeks. You need to get some ideas for a great experiment.

    a. A Science Fair Project Resource Guide

       http://www.ipl.org/youth/projectguide/

    b. Complete Guide to Science Projects

       http://members.web.com/ScienzFair/ideas

    c. The Kid's Guide to Hands-On Science

       http://www.ucandoscience.com

_____

_____

4. A book that you checked out from the school library has a big silver seal on it that says "Newbery." Your librarian explains that the book is a Newbery Award winner. You want to find out more about this award.

    a. History of Children's Book Awards

       http://www.jefferson.com/awards

    b. The Newbery Award

       http://www.ala.org/alsc/newbery.html

    c. Best of Children's Literature—Newbery Winners

       http://libpage.com/george/best/newbery

_____

_____

5. You learned about ancient Egyptian culture in class. You know that many Egyptian gods appear both as people and animals. You're curious to learn more about Egyptian gods.

    a. Life in Ancient Egypt: Gods and Religion

       http://www.carnegiemuseums.org/cmnh/exhibits/egypt/religion.html

    b. Egyptian Gods

       http://users.aol.com/asmith/egyptiangods.html

    c. My Favorite Egyptian Gods

       http://www.anubishome.com/godsimages.html

_____

_____

Choosing CD-ROM Databases

CD-ROM database sources are another way to get information in the library. This may also be a tool you can use in your classroom or at home. A database is contained on a CD-ROM, and it is sort of like an electronic encyclopedia. A database may contain old newspaper or magazine articles; it may contain photos, dictionaries, or encyclopedias. Just as with books and online sources, you need to know the best sources to choose.

➤ **Look at the titles of the CD-ROM databases in the box below. Choose which one you would use for each of the following research questions and write the title on the line.**

> 1. ProQuest Resource/One—130 periodicals (magazine articles)
>
> 2. SIRS Researcher—social sciences database (health, science, and environmental articles)
>
> 3. CD NewsBank—100+ newspapers (U.S. and international)
>
> 4. McGraw-Hill Multimedia Encyclopedia of Science and Technology (encyclopedia-style articles)

1. Where did the most recent oil spill take place?

_____

2. What are the latest treatments available for bone cancer?

_____

3. What is Italy doing about water pollution?

_____

4. What is the future of the electric car?

_____

5. What is the current U.S. President's view on recycling?

_____

6. When did Russian and American astronauts first travel in space together?

_____

7. What is the favorite pet of most Americans?

_____

Selecting Sample History Databases

Read the descriptions of the history database examples on page 48, and then analyze the research questions below. Choose one database to start a computer search for each question. Write the title on the line provided. (Note: The databases listed are fictitious but your library may have CD-ROM databases with similar information.)

1. Where can you find a speech given by President Lincoln? _____
   _____

2. Why is Martin Luther King, Jr. a famous American? _____
   _____

3. Is Mt. Rushmore in the national list of famous places? _____

4. Who fired the first shot in the American Revolution? _____

5. Where can you find a map of Poland? _____

6. How did the Plains Indians build their homes? _____

7. Did President Jefferson make a speech when he won the election? _____
   _____

8. Is there a newspaper article on the first American in space? _____
   _____

9. Where can you find a map of the United States? _____

10. Where can you find information on Malcolm X? _____

Name _____ Date _____

History Database Examples

Encyclopedia of Native Americans
Covers tribes, locations, and customs.

Encyclopedia of the American Revolution
Covers the period from colonization to the end of the revolution.

Atlas of U.S. Presidents
Includes biographies as well as speeches of all U.S. Presidents.

World History Fact Book
Covers world history and includes maps, photographs, and animation.

U.S. History
Reports on historical figures and major events with newspaper coverage.

African-American History
Covers U.S. history and the civil rights movement to the present time.

Famous Places
Covers unusual or famous places throughout the world.

History of Europe
Covers the culture and history of all countries in Europe through 2000.

History and Culture of South America
Covers the culture and history of South American countries.

Presidents
Includes portraits, biographies, election results, maps, essays, and timelines.

The American Constitution
Explains the origins of the American Constitution.
Includes biographies of historical figures involved in its making.

U.S. Geography
Covers states and their capitals. Many detailed maps included.

The Elections
Explains the process of participating in U.S. elections.

Name _____ Date _____

Choosing Topics

Read the following sets of research topics. Write *broad* if the topic is too general. Write *specific* if the topic is too narrow. Write *good* if the topic would work well for a report.

broad?

specific?

good?

1. a. the Solar System _____

   b. Jupiter's Colors _____

   c. the Planet Jupiter _____

2. a. Sir Francis Drake's Boat _____

   b. Explorers _____

   c. Sir Francis Drake _____

3. a. Taking Care of Your Dog _____

   b. Feeding Your Dog _____

   c. Raising Pets _____

4. a. Native-American Tribes of North America _____

   b. the Arapaho _____

   c. Arapaho Tools _____

5. a. the History of Baseball _____

   b. Babe Ruth _____

   c. the Role of the First Baseman in Baseball _____

6. a. Cooking Around the World _____

   b. French Cheeses—How They Are Made _____

   c. French Toast _____

7. a. the King Cobra _____

   b. Snakes _____

   c. the Snake's Digestive System _____

8. a. How a Sailboat Works _____

   b. a Boat's Rudder _____

   c. Boats _____

 0-7424-1956-8 *Complete Library Skills*

Picking the Best Topic

➡ **Read the following sets of research topics. Write** *broad* **if the topic is too general. Write** *specific* **if the topic is too narrow. Write** *good* **if the topic would work well for a report.**

1. a. Black Death _____

    b. Treatment of Black Death _____

    c. The Middle Ages _____

2. a. Cowboys: Saddles & Equipment _____

    b. Cowboys _____

    c. the Rodeo _____

3. a. Life in Quebec _____

    b. Life in Canada _____

    c. Food in Quebec _____

4. a. a Plant's Roots _____

    b. Parts of the Plant _____

    c. Plants _____

5. a. the Victorian Music Hall _____

    b. Victorian Entertainment _____

    c. the Victorian Age _____

6. a. Prehistoric _____

    b. Weapons _____

    c. the Samurai Dagger _____

7. a. Caves _____

    b. How Caves Form _____

    c. Stalagmites _____

broad?
specific?
good?

Analyzing a Research Question

▶ **Think of an area of interest that you would like to research. Answer the questions below to prepare for your information search. Write your answers on the lines provided.**

I. What topic would you like to research? _____

_____

2. What research question could you use to locate information for your topic?

_____

_____

3. Analyze your question. Is it general or specific? If it's general, rewrite the question to make it more specific.

_____

_____

4. What are the keywords to help research your question? _____

_____

5. Can any of the keywords be combined to create narrow search terms? Write them here. _____

_____

_____

Forming Research Questions

▶ Look at the web below. It lists a broad topic and a few subtopics. Fill in the other ovals with other subtopics and details or questions. What do you want to know about dinosaurs?

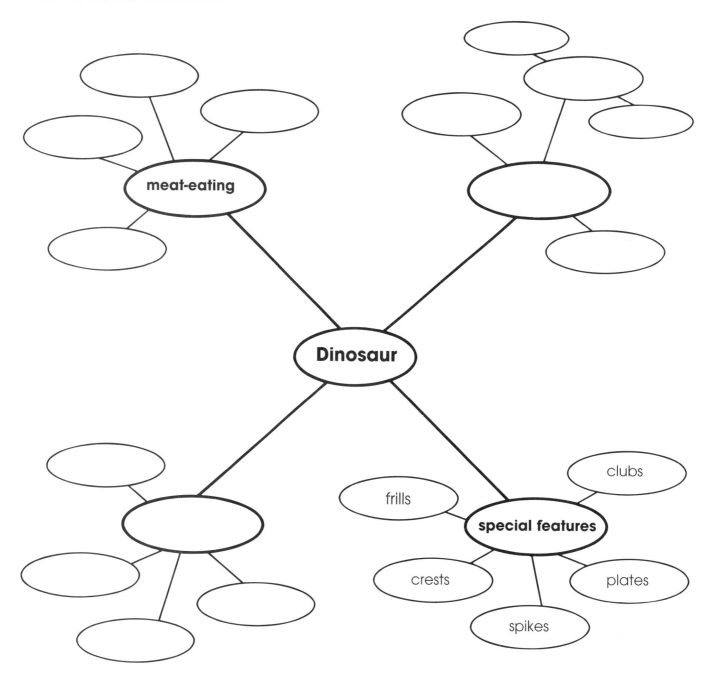

▶ Use this kind of web to brainstorm questions about a topic that interests you.

Name _____ Date _____

Preliminary Research Checklist

➤ **Before you finish your preliminary research, use the checklist below to make sure that you have explored all sources that may be helpful to you. When you have completed the checklist, let the *real* research begin!**

- ☐ I have looked under my topic name in at least two encyclopedias.
- ☐ I have looked at the books containing information on my topic name in the library.
- ☐ I have used the Reader's Guide for looking up magazine articles.
- ☐ I have asked the librarian if he or she knows of any helpful sources for my report.
- ☐ I have done a quick keyword search on the Web.

Yes	No	
☐	☐	Will the almanac be helpful?
☐	☐	Will the atlas be helpful?
☐	☐	Will the biographical dictionary be helpful?
☐	☐	Will the vertical file be helpful?
☐	☐	Can I find information on the Web?
☐	☐	Does the library have any relevant CD-ROM databases?

Using a Magazine Guide—Hobbies

Hobbies

"All About Baseball." *Sports Digest.* Oct. 15, 1997.

"All About Chess." *Hobby Magazine.* May 6, 1999.

"Baseball Card Collecting." *Hobby Magazine.* May 19, 1997.

"Coin Collecting." *Hobby Digest.* Aug. 3, 2000.

"Dolls: Making Clothes." *Hobby Digest.* Jul. 13, 2000.

"Football for Teens." *Sports Digest.* Jul. 13, 1999.

"Painting for Kids." *Arts and Crafts Magazine.* Apr. 17, 2001.

"Stamp Collecting." *Hobby Digest.* Apr. 7, 2002.

"Stamps of the World: Building Your Collection." *Stamp World.* Jun. 16, 2000.

"Water Color Painting for Young People." *Arts and Crafts.* Apr. 17, 1999.

Read the magazine guide. Answer the questions.

1. In which article can you find information about collecting baseball cards?

_____

2. You found a stamp on an old envelope. What article may help you find what country it is from? _____

3. Where can you find information about football? _____

4. Your uncle plays chess. You don't. What article might help? _____

5. What two articles will tell you about painting?_____

6. What article will help you make a new set of doll clothes? _____

7. You need more information about baseball. _____

8. Your cousin collects coins. What article will give you more information? _____

_____

9. What article was written for young people about football? _____

10. What two articles are about stamps? _____

Using a Magazine Guide—Cooking

Cooking

"Baking for Kids." *Cooking Magazine.* Oct. 11, 2001.

"Cookies for Holidays." *Cookie Digest.* Oct. 17, 2000.

"Cakes for Special Occasions." *Cooking Digest.* Dec. 19, 1999.

"Cooking and Nutrition." *Health Magazine.* Sept. 21, 2000.

"Decorating Cakes." *Cooking Digest.* Oct. 20, 1997.

"Making Dinner." *Health Magazine.* Mar. 20, 1999.

"Making Lunch." *Health Magazine.* May 19, 2003.

"Making Salads." *Health Magazine.* Oct. 13, 1998.

"Making Soups." *Health Magazine.* Apr. 13, 2001.

"Vitamins and Cooking." *Health Magazine.* Nov. 21, 2002.

▶ **Read the magazine guide. Answer the questions.**

1. Where would you find help to bake a cake for your sister's birthday?_____

   _____

2. Is it a good idea to mix rice and beans to make a nutritious dish? What article will help you? _____

3. How does cooking your food affect its vitamins? _____

4. Help! You need tips on decorating the cake you just made. _____

5. Are there any good recipes for baking that are just for kids? _____

6. How do you make a recipe for a school party? _____

7. You need a special recipe for dinner. _____

8. You need a cookie recipe for a school party. _____

9. What article is written just for kids? _____

10. What two articles will help you with nutrition? _____

Termite Book Index

Termites

▶ **Read the index. Write the page number of where you would look.**

1. How do you know if your house has termites? _____

2. Do termites really eat wood? _____

3. Are ants related to termites? _____

4. Are ladybugs and termites friends? _____

5. How many legs does a termite have? _____

6. Is *flying ant* another name for a termite? _____

7. What do termites eat? _____

8. Do termites live in wood? _____

9. Are spiders related to termites? _____

10. Can you find termites in the dark? _____

Toy Book Index

Toys

▶ **Read the index. Answer the questions. Write the page number.**

1. Where will you find information about teddy bears? _____

2. Is a kite a toy? _____

3. When was the first train made? _____

4. What are easy toys that you can make at home? _____

5. What are common toys for children? _____

6. What materials do you need to make a dollhouse? _____

7. With what types of toys did the colonists play? _____

8. Did the children of the wild west have toys? _____

9. Where was the first train made? _____

10. Can kites that fly be made at home? _____

Using an Almanac

Baseball

Addresses of teams	820
All Star games	865
All-Time leaders	881
Batting records	869–880
Home runs	868
Little League series	876
Pitching records	870, 874
World Series	877

Space Developments

Apollo trips	168–169
Astronauts	169–170
Cosmonauts	168–169
First person in space	168
First space walk	168
Mars landing	484
Moonwalk, U.S.	169, 482
Space shuttle	170, 486

Television

Actors, Actresses	399–415
Awards	350–359
Favorite U.S. programs	372, 373
Sets, number of	373
Time spent viewing	372
Video cassette recorders	97

▶ **Read the almanac index above. On what pages will you find answers to these questions?**

1. How many television sets are there in the U.S.? _____

2. What is the average time Americans spend watching television? _____

3. Who was part of the space shuttle Discovery crew? _____

4. Who was the first person in space? _____

5. Who was the first American in space? _____

6. What is the address of the Los Angeles Dodgers? _____

7. Who hit the most home runs in 1996? _____

8. What was the score of the All Star Game in 1996? _____

9. Where can you find information about television awards? _____

10. How many videocassette recorders are there in the U.S.? _____

Almanac Review

Animals

Cat breeds	156
Collection of animal names	154
Endangered species	153
Farm animals	154
Major poisonous animals	155
Speed of animals	154
Wildlife animals	149
Zoo animals	156

➤ **Read the almanac index. On what pages will you find answers to these questions?**

1. Is the giant panda on the endangered species list? _____

2. Is it true that the cheetah can run 60 mph? _____

3. Is it true that the stingray is a poisonous animal? _____

4. How many zoos are there in the U.S.? _____

5. Is the ocelot on the endangered species list? _____

6. How many animals are in the Bronx Zoo? _____

7. How many cat breeds are there? _____

8. Is *band* the name of a collection of gorillas? _____

9. Is the Gila monster a poisonous lizard? _____

10. Is it true the poisonous rattlesnake is 2–8 feet long? _____

Name _____ Date _____

Using a Biographical Dictionary

▶ **Read the biographical dictionary entry for George Washington below. Then answer the questions.**

Washington, George. 1732–1799. First President of the United States, born Westmoreland County, VA, eldest son of Augustine Washington (death 1743), a Virginia planter, and his second wife, Mary Ball (1708–89). Privately educated. County surveyor, Culpeper County, VA (1749). Inherited Mount Vernon after death of Lawrence (1752). Served on General Braddock's staff (1755). Married Martha Custis (Jan. 6, 1759), widow of Daniel Parke Custis; retired to Mount Vernon to live life of Virginia gentleman-farmer. Member of first and second Continental Congress (1774-75). Elected to command all Continental armies (June 5, 1775); won the battle of Princeton; established headquarters at Morristown, NJ (1777). Resigned commission (Dec. 23, 1783) and again retired to Mount Vernon to resume care of the plantation.

Called from retirement to preside at federal convention in Philadelphia (1787). Unanimously chosen as President of the United States under the new constitution; took oath of office in New York City (Apr. 30, 1789). Retired from political life (March 3, 1797). On threat of war with France (1798), accepted commission until his death (Dec. 14, 1799). Buried in tomb on his estate at Mount Vernon. Elected to American Hall of Fame (1900).

1. Why did Washington not serve a third term as president? _____
   _____

2. When was Washington elected to the American Hall of Fame? _____

3. Where did he take the oath of office? _____

4. What did Washington do after his first retirement? _____

5. Did he win the battle of Princeton? _____

6. Where was Washington born? _____

7. In what country was Washington a surveyor? _____

8. When was he a member of the first and second Continental Congress? _____
   _____

9. Was he ever commander in chief of the Virginia troops? _____

10. Where did he establish his headquarters in 1777? _____

Name _____ Date _____

Using an Encyclopedia Index

Encyclopedia of Transportation		
Transportation		
Automobile	A-61	
Busses	B-3	
Cars	C-81	
Helicopters	H-91	
Submarines	S-135	
Trains	T-147	
Trolley cars	T-189	

Encyclopedia of Travel		
Transportation		
Automobile	A-36	
Airplanes	A-89	
Antique Cars	A-91	
Balloons, Hot Air	B-367	
Boats	B-411	
Jets	J-502	
Sailboats	S-496	
Speedboats	S-431	

Read each index above. Answer the questions. When necessary write the name of the encyclopedia, the volume, and page number.

1. Where can you find information about sailboats? _____

2. Can you find information about trolley cars in both indices? _____

3. On what page can you find information about submarines? _____

4. On what page can you find information about airplanes? _____

5. Can you find information about helicopters in both indices? _____

6. What types of boats can you find information about? _____

7. Where can you find information about antique cars? _____

8. Are there two entries for automobiles? _____

9. Can you find information about hot air balloons? _____ Where? _____

10. Can you find information about jets in both indices? _____

Name _____ Date _____

Comparing Encyclopedia Indices

Encyclopedia of the World

Hobbies

Arts and crafts	A-305
Basketball	B-401
Coins, collecting	C-275
Dancing	D-117
Dolls, collecting	D-87
Football	F-301
Hockey	H-565
Karate	K-411
Stamps, collecting	S-329

Encyclopedia of Knowledge

Hobbies

Baseball	B-367
Chess	C-63
Drawing	D-17
Ice hockey	I-309
Judo	J-287
Painting	P-111
Swimming	S-117
Water sports	W-294

▶ **Read each index above. Compare. Answer the questions.**

1. Where would you find information about collecting stamps? _____

2. What encyclopedia has information about karate? _____

3. Can you find information about chess in both indices? _____

4. Can you find information about water sports in both indices? _____

5. Is there any information about hockey? _____ Where? _____

6. Is there information about basketball? _____ Where? _____

7. Is there information about ice hockey? _____ Where _____

8. What are the names of the entries about art? _____

9. Where can you find information about swimming? _____

10. Can you find information about drawing in both indices? _____

How to Read Charts, Time Lines, and Tables

While you are reading for information on your topic, you will likely come to some charts, tables, and time lines. These should not be passed over as unimportant information. If you take the time to study them, these visuals will show you in a vivid, graphic style how facts and ideas relate to one another and how conclusions can be drawn from what you have learned in your reading.

Finding Information from Charts

In order to understand a chart you have to be able to read one correctly. Look at the four basic steps below.

1. Find the basic idea or information that the chart is presenting. You can get this information quickly by checking the title.

2. Break down the large topic into smaller parts of information. You can get this information quickly by checking the titles of each column.

3. Read carefully the details or smaller parts of information in the columns. You can get this information by starting at the top and working through the chart.

4. Understand the information you have studied on the chart. Draw conclusions based on the information that the chart is presenting.

Endangered Species Chart

Some Endangered Species of Animals

Common Name	Scientific Name	Distribution	Survival Problem
American crocodile	*Crocodylus*	Florida, Mexico, Central and South Caribbean islands, and India	Over-hunted for its hide; habitat destruction
Asiatic lion	*Panthera leo persica*	India	Habitat destruction; over-hunted for sport
Black-footed ferret	*Mustela nigripes*	Known only in captivity	Poisoning of prairie dogs, its chief prey
Black rhinoceros	*Diceros biocornis*	South of Sahara in Africa	Habitat destruction; over-hunted for its horn
Blue whale	*Balaenoptera musculus*	All oceans	Over-hunted for its blubber (for food and for whale oil)
Brown pelican	*Pelecanus occidentalis*	North Carolina to Texas, California, West Indies, and coastal Central and South America	Contamination of food supply by pesticides
California condor	*Gymnogyps Californianus*	Known only in captivity	Habitat destruction; hunted for sport; over-collection of eggs for food
Devils Hole pupfish	*Cyprinodon diabolis*	Nevada	Habitat destruction
Imperial parrot	*Amazona imperialis*	West Indies and Dominica	Habitat destruction; illegal capture for pets

▶ **Read the chart above. Answer the questions.**

1. What are the four sections of information presented in this chart? _____

_____

2. What is the scientific name of the blue whale? _____

3. What are the survival problems of the black rhinoceros? _____

_____

4. Where does the Asiatic lion live? _____

5. What is the range of the American crocodile? _____

6. *Mustela nigripes* is the scientific name for what animal? _____

7. What two animals are known in captivity only? _____

8. What animal has been captured for pets? _____

Space Probes Chart

Important Space Probes

Date Launched	Name	Launched by	Accomplishments
1959 Sept. 12	*Luna 2*	U.S.S.R.*	First probe to strike the moon
1962 Apr. 23	*Ranger 4*	U.S.A.	First probe to strike the moon; failed to televise pictures to Earth
1964 Nov. 28	*Mariner 4*	U.S.A.	Photographed Mars on Jul. 14, 1965; measured conditions in space
1966 Jan. 31	*Luna 9*	U.S.S.R.	Made first soft landing on the moon on Feb. 3; sent 27 pictures to Earth
1966 Mar. 31	*Luna 10*	U.S.S.R.	First spacecraft to orbit the moon; began orbiting on Apr. 3
1967 Jun. 12	*Venera 4*	U.S.S.R.	First spacecraft to transmit data about Venus's atmosphere
1968 Sept. 14	*Zond 5*	U.S.S.R.	First probe to orbit the moon and return to a soft landing on Earth
1970 Aug. 17	*Venera 7*	U.S.S.R.	First spacecraft to transmit data from Venus's surface; landed Dec. 15, 1970
1970 Sept. 12	*Luna 16*	U.S.S.R.	First unmanned spacecraft to return lunar samples; landed Sept. 20
1971 May 28	*Mars 3*	U.S.S.R.	Carried capsule that made first soft landing on Mars; landed Dec. 2, 1971
1971 May 30	*Mariner 9*	U.S.A.	First probe to orbit Mars; began orbiting on Nov. 13
1972 Mar. 2	*Pioneer 10*	U.S.A.	Flew past Jupiter on Dec. 3, 1973, and sent back scientific data; on Jun. 13, 1983, became the first spacecraft to travel beyond all the planets

*U.S.S.R.= Union of Soviet Socialist Republics (a country made up of Russia and other Eastern European states)

▶ **Read the chart above. Answer the questions.**

1. What are the four sections presented in this chart? _____

_____

2. What spacecraft made the first soft landing on the moon? _____

3. What was the first spacecraft to orbit the moon?_____

4. The *Luna 16* was launched on what date?_____

5. What country sent the first probe to Mars? _____

6. On April 23, 1962, the United States sent what spacecraft to the moon?_____

7. What was the first spacecraft to transmit data on Venus's atmosphere?_____

8. The *Pioneer 10* flew past what planet in 1973?_____

Name _____ Date _____

Reading a Time Line

Early Explorers

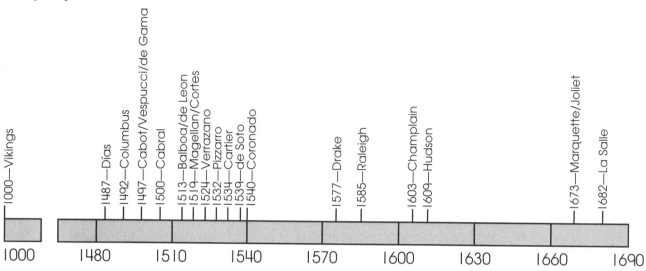

Read the time line. Answer the questions.

1. What time period does this time line cover? _____

2. What is the date for Drake? _____

3. What is the date for La Salle? _____

4. Is 1608 the correct date for Champlain? _____

5. Between what two major dates did most of the exploration take place?

_____

6. In what year are both Balboa and de Leon given credit for early explorations?

_____

7. Name the two explorers in the 1570–1600 time period. _____

8. Between what two major dates did no major explorations take place? _____

_____

9. Name the explorers in the 1660–1690 time period? _____

_____

Name _____ Date _____

Using Time Line Information

World War I

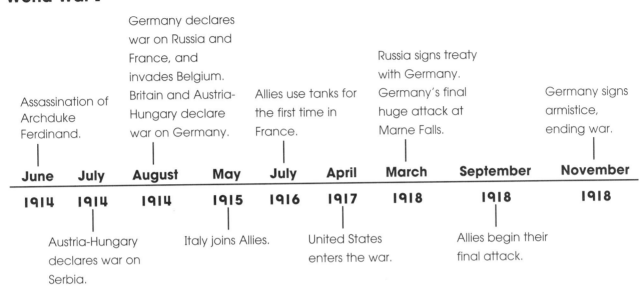

Allies begin their final attack.

▶ **Read the time line. Answer the questions.**

1. What time period does this time line cover? _____

2. What month and year was Archduke Ferdinand assassinated? _____

3. What two events took place in March 1918? _____

_____

4. Who began their final attack in September 1918? _____

5. When did Britain and Austria-Hungary declare war on Germany? _____

_____

6. What major event took place in July 1916? _____

_____

7. When did the United States enter World War I? _____

8. When did Italy enter the war? _____

9. What major event took place in November 1918? _____

_____

Name _____ Date _____

Finding Information in a Table

Super Bowl

Year	Winner	Loser	Site
1967	Green Bay Packers, 35	Kansas City Chiefs, 10	Los Angeles Coliseum
1968	Green Bay Packers, 33	Oakland Raiders, 14	Orange Bowl, Miami
1969	New York Jets, 16	Baltimore Colts, 7	Orange Bowl, Miami
1970	Kansas City Chiefs, 23	Minnesota Vikings, 7	Tulane Stadium, New Orleans
1971	Baltimore Colts, 16	Dallas Cowboys, 13	Orange Bowl, Miami
1972	Dallas Cowboys, 24	Miami Dolphins, 3	Tulane Stadium, New Orleans
1973	Miami Dolphins, 14	Washington Redskins, 7	Los Angeles Coliseum
1974	Miami Dolphins, 24	Minnesota Vikings, 7	Rice Stadium, Houston
1975	Pittsburgh Steelers, 16	Minnesota Vikings, 6	Tulane Stadium, New Orleans
1976	Pittsburgh Steelers, 21	Dallas Cowboys, 17	Orange Bowl, Miami
1977	Oakland Raiders, 32	Minnesota Vikings, 14	Rose Bowl, Pasadena

▶ **Read the table. Answer the questions.**

1. What four sections are presented in the Super Bowl table? _____

_____

_____

2. Who was the winner in 1975? _____

3. What was the score for the 1967 game? _____

4. Who played against the New York Jets in 1969? _____

5. In what year did the Minnesota Vikings play against the Kansas City Chiefs?

_____

Name _____ Date _____

Tables Are Helpful

Fastest Scheduled Train Runs in United States and Canada

Railroad	Train	From	To	Dis. (miles)	Time (min.)	Speed (mph)
Amtrak	Three Metroliners	Baltimore	Wilmington	68.4	42	97.8
Amtrak	Metroliner 101	Metro Park	Prince Junction	23.9	15	95.6
Amtrak	Eight Metroliners	Baltimore	Wilmington	68.4	43	95.4
Amtrak	Three Metroliners	Wilmington	Baltimore	68.4	45	91.2
Amtrak	Eight Metroliners	Wilmington	Baltimore	68.4	46	89.2
Amtrak	Four trains	Rensselaer	Hudson	28.0	19	88.4
Amtrak	Three Metroliners	Newark	Philadelphia	80.5	56	86.2
Amtrak	Three trains	Baltimore	Wilmington	68.4	48	85.5
Amtrak	Garden State Special	Aberdeen	Wilmington	38.3	27	85.1
Amtrak	Two Metroliners	Metro Park	Philadelphia	66.4	47	84.8
Amtrak	Virginian	Trenton	Metro Park	33.9	34	84.7
Amtrak	Five Metroliners	Newark	Philadelphia	80.5	57	84.7
Amtrak	Three trains	Baltimore	Wilmington	68.4	48	83.8
Amtrak	Three Metroliners	Philadelphia	Newark	80.5	58	83.3
Amtrak	Independence	Newark (Del)	Baltimore	56.8	47	83.1
Via Rail Canada	Five trains	Guildwood	Kingston	145.1	105	82.9

► **Read the table. Answer the questions.**

1. What seven sections are listed in this table? _____

_____

2. How is the distance measured in this table? _____

3. What are the two railroads listed? _____

4. How is time measured in this table? _____

5. What is the time listed for the Independence train? _____

6. From where does the Virginian leave? _____

7. What is the speed (mph) of the Garden State Special? _____

8. The Three Metroliners leave Baltimore and arrive where? _____

Name _____ Date _____

Learn How to Skim

Skimming is a technique you can use in your preliminary research as you are deciding which sources you want to use for your report.

When you skim you read quickly through an article or chapter and try to understand the main idea and key points without slowing down for details.

Skimming is an especially helpful reading technique when you are exploring a lengthy article or chapter on your topic.

By skimming—reading much faster than you would at a normal speed—you can get an overall feel for what is important in the material quickly so that you can move on to investigation of your next source.

 Skim paragraph 1 below. Then record five important points (on the next page) that you remember from skimming the paragraph. Then skim paragraph 2 and record five key points that you remember from this paragraph.

Paragraph 1

How do you bake cookies? First, put all the ingredients out on the table. This makes it easy to begin. Second, read the recipe carefully. Do you have all the ingredients that you need? Now set the oven to the temperature for which the recipe calls. It is important to have the oven hot for the cookies to bake well. Next mix the ingredients as the recipe tells you. Shape the cookies and put them on a flat sheet. Bake. Then cool the cookies. That's how you bake cookies.

Paragraph 2

How do you choose a book for your report? First, learn exactly what the assignment will be. If you do this it will help you to know what to look for. Next, ask yourself how long the book must be. Often, your teachers will give you an idea of how many pages you must read. Also, ask yourself what type of book you need to choose. Do you need a mystery book, a biography, or a science fiction book? Now you can check the shelves. When you find a book that interests you, do three things. Read the dust jacket. This will give you an idea of the book's contents. Skim the table of contents. This will give you information about the book. Check the author. Is it an author whose other books you have read and liked? Now check out your book!

Learn How to Skim (cont.)

▶ **Skim the paragraphs on page 70. Write five details for each paragraph.**

Paragraph 1

1. _____
   _____

2. _____
   _____

3. _____
   _____

4. _____
   _____

5. _____
   _____

Paragraph 2

1. _____
   _____

2. _____
   _____

3. _____
   _____

4. _____
   _____

5. _____
   _____

Name _____ Date _____

Skim to Get the Main Idea

▶ **Use with the article on page 73.**

1. Skim the title and the first three paragraphs. What is the main idea or purpose of this article? _____

_____

_____

_____

2. Skim the article again from the beginning to the end. Write down at least four details. These can be words or phrases that you notice.

_____

_____

_____

_____

3. Now read the whole article and write a summary that is no more than four sentences long. Did your skimming help? Were you right about the main idea?

_____

_____

_____

_____

_____

_____

 Use with the activities on page 72.

Can you tell the difference between a crocodile and an alligator? Or do you think that they look pretty much alike?

Both the crocodile and the alligator belong to a group of reptiles called crocodilians. All crocodilians have cigar-shaped bodies and look like giant lizards. All have tough skin made up of hard, bony plates and scales.

Crocodiles and alligators have even more in common than their shapes and skin. They have short legs and long, powerful tails that they sweep from side to side when swimming. Both are good swimmers. They eat mostly fish, birds, turtles, and snakes, and any small mammals they can catch. Large males of both species have been known to attack larger animals such as dogs and cattle. They have even attacked people. Alligators drag their prey underwater until they drown. Then they tear them to pieces. Crocodiles latch into their prey. Then they twist them into pieces by spinning lengthwise very rapidly in the water.

The best way to tell a crocodile from an alligator is to look at its snout. The snout of the crocodile is narrow. It nearly comes to a point at the tip. The snout of an alligator is wider. It is round at the end. The crocodile is also lighter, quicker, and meaner than the alligator. It is not unusual for some types of crocodiles to leave the water and attack people. The alligator normally will not attack humans unless it is hungry or provoked.

Crocodiles are found on every continent except Europe and Antarctica. Alligators, except for a kind that is native to eastern China, are limited to the Americas. In the United States, they live in swamps, rivers, and coastal areas of several southern states.

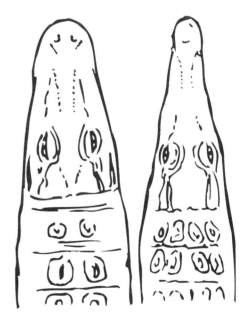

Learn to Free Write

After you have completed your preliminary research and have looked up information on your topic in several sources, you are able to free write.

In many ways free writing is like brainstorming. When you free write you write about everything concerning your topic that you can remember reading about during your preliminary research.

Unlike brainstorming, however, you already have your topic. Now you need to come up with ideas of what you want to discuss about your topic in your paper. Write down whatever comes to mind: phrases, comparisons, thoughts, and questions especially—anything having to do with your topic. As with brainstorming, do not worry about spelling, grammar, or penmanship.

➡ **The following example of free writing has been started for you. Write down questions or thoughts you have about this topic.**

Topic: Falcons

What do falcons eat? Where do they live? Falcons as pets; falconing.

_____

_____

_____

_____

_____

_____

_____

_____

_____

_____

_____

Name _____ Date _____

Free Writing

➤ **Look at this question.**

Why do we have speed limits?

Use the prompts below to help you start free writing about this topic.

1. Why do you think many people drive over the speed limit?

_____

_____

_____

2. Why do most roads have posted speed limits?

_____

_____

_____

3. Suggest an alternative to speed limits.

_____

_____

_____

4. Why do you think many cars are built to travel faster than speed limits allow?

_____

_____

_____

_____

Note Taking Tips

When you first start taking notes, you may have a difficult time writing them down correctly. The following tips should help you.

1. Read the entire article or chapter before you start taking any notes—it's best to get an overview of what you are reading first to make sure you only take notes on what you need.

2. Go back over the material and carefully select the information you want to include in your report. Stick with your chosen topic. Unless something seems very important, try to take notes only on information that answers the questions you wrote down during your free writing.

3. Label each note card at the top with the subheading or the questions that it answers.

4. When you come to a fact or an idea that you think will be helpful in your report, close the book or magazine you are reading, think about what you have read, and then write down the fact or information in your own words. By closing the book before you take your notes, you ensure that you've understood what you've read; this also is a safeguard against copying straight out of the book. Copying the exact words out of a book is called *plagiarism.* This is illegal. You must use your own words.

5. Facts, measurements, dates, or other statistics are okay to copy. This information belongs to everyone. Make sure that you use these facts in sentences in your own words and that you copy the facts correctly.

6. If you find a paragraph that you want to take notes on, it is best to sum up the paragraph in just two or three sentences in a way that the paragraph makes sense to you. Shortening a full paragraph into a few sentences in your own words is called *paraphrasing* or *summarizing.*

7. If you want to use the author's words exactly as they are written (you may want to do this if the author is expressing an opinion), copy them with the page number where they are found. When you write this quotation in your report, you will put these borrowed words in quotation marks.

3 x 5 Reproducible Note Taking Cards

Source:

Subheading/Topic:

Source:

Subheading/Topic:

4 x 6 Reproducible Note Taking Cards

Source:

Topic:

Question/Subheading:

Source:

Topic:

Question/Subheading:

Bibliography Note Taking Cards

Book Bibliography Card

Author:

Title:

Place of publication:

Publisher:

Copyright date:

Pages:

Encyclopedia Bibliography Card

Author:

Title:

Name of encyclopedia:

Copyright date:

Volume:

Pages:

Magazine Bibliography Card

Author (if given):

Title of article:

Name of magazine:

Volume number:

Date:

Pages:

Name _____   Date _____

Venture to Venus

➤ **Take notes on the following selection. Use the outline on page 81 to organize your thoughts.**

Venus is the second planet from the sun. It is slightly smaller than Earth, with a diameter of about 7,500 miles (12,068 km).

Volcanic eruptions have covered much of the surface with lava flows. It is a barren planet with huge plains and lowlands. There are two important highland areas, Aphrodite Terra, which is about the size of Africa; and Ishtar Terra, similar in size to Australia. The highest point on Venus is in the Maxwell Montes on Ishtar. It includes a peak that soars 7 miles (11 km) above the surface.

The atmosphere of Venus is made up mostly of carbon dioxide. It acts like a blanket to keep in heat, and the temperatures may reach 900° F (482° C)—that is hot enough to melt lead! Atmospheric pressure at the surface of the planet is 90 times greater than that of Earth. Venus is covered with a layer of clouds of sulfuric acid, which lead to acid rain, most of which probably evaporates in the extreme heat before it reaches the surface.

Venus spins in the opposite direction of Earth. That means that on Venus the sun rises in the west and sets in the east. It spins very slowly, taking 243 Earth days to make one complete turn on its axis. Since Venus completes one orbit around the sun in 225 Earth days, a day on Venus is longer than its year.

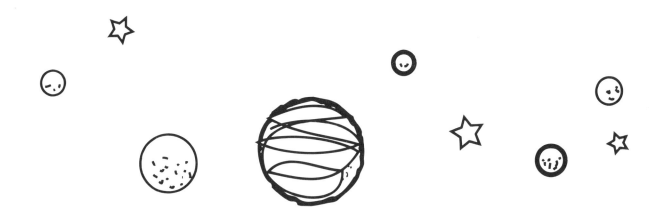

0-7424-1956-8 *Complete Library Skills*

Title: _____

I. Main idea _____

   A. Subtopic _____

      1. Subtopic detail _____

      2. Subtopic detail _____

   B. Subtopic _____

      1. Subtopic detail _____

      2. Subtopic detail _____

II. Main idea _____

   A. Subtopic _____

      1. Subtopic detail _____

      2. Subtopic detail _____

   B. Subtopic _____

      1. Subtopic detail _____

      2. Subtopic detail _____

III. Main idea _____

   A. Subtopic _____

      1. Subtopic detail _____

      2. Subtopic detail _____

Outlining Tips

The following tips should help you create accurate and complete outlines.

1. Include only the key points in your outline. Do not list any of the minute details until you actually write your report.

2. You may want to do more than one outline before you write your report. The first "rough" outline would be the most basic with only one or two-word phrases labeling each section. A second outline will be more specific and have more facts filled in. Your third outline might be very close to what your actual report would look like. Remember: The better and more detailed your outline, the easier it will be to write your report.

3. No matter how detailed your outline, always leave the specific, supporting details out—they will clutter the outline.

4. You probably took more notes than you included in your outline. Be selective in your writing—you do not need to include everything from your notes.

5. In your conclusion you will either:

   a. Sum up, or repeat the main idea.

   b. Give your personal opinion on the topic, or

   c. Give a "predictive" closing. (You would likely use this type of conclusion with a current-event related topic.)

You might start your conclusion with words like, "therefore," "finally," "in conclusion," etc.

Name _____ Date _____

Sample Outlining Diagram

Introduction

General opening sentence to lead into report topic

I. Introduction to "Life in France"

1st Main Idea

II. Daily Activities
  1. School
  2. Entertainment

2nd Main Idea

III. Foods
  1. Cheese
  2. Main dishes
  3. Desserts

3rd Main Idea

IV. Going to Paris
  1. Eiffel Tower
  2. Louvre Museum
  3. Arc de Triomphe

Conclusion

V. Conclusion

A Man Remembered

Read the following information and then fill in the character web on page 85.

Benjamin Franklin is one of the most important people in American history. The influence of his life has stayed with us for over 200 years. Today we see his picture on stamps and on the hundred-dollar bill. Just why is this man still remembered?

Franklin was one of 17 children. He was born to a very poor family in Boston, Massachusetts. He did not get a very good education. His father could not afford to send him to school past his tenth birthday. However, Franklin did not stop learning. He taught himself reading, writing, math, different languages, science, and philosophy through books. When he was 17 years old, Franklin moved to Philadelphia.

Within a couple years, Franklin owned a printing business. He then printed a newspaper. He earned great fame publishing a yearly book called an almanac. It included poems, financial advice, jokes, and even predicted the weather. It sold around the world.

Although Franklin thought that printing was his career, he was known for much more. Whenever he saw a problem, Benjamin Franklin set out to invent a solution. His inventions include an energy-efficient wood-burning stove and bifocal glasses. He established an academy of learning. He started the first city hospital. He had many other ideas that improved life for the citizens of Philadelphia. He did not ask for money. He simply wished to make life better for people.

Franklin also played an important role in the making of America. He helped bring an end to the Revolutionary War. Then he took part in the Constitutional Convention. Benjamin Franklin died at the age of 84. We still remember him today over 200 years later.

A Man Remembered (cont.)

▶ **Fill in the character web below with details about what you read on page 84.**

1. Childhood and Education

3. What did he print?

Benjamin Franklin

2. Where do we still see him?

4. Inventions and Improvements

▶ **Using the web, rewrite the passage in your own words on a separate sheet of paper. You may look at the web as needed. However, try not to look back at the article once you have started writing.**

The Budding Scientist

Read the story. Then fill in the web on page 87.

On Wednesday, Malik Ford was worried. Two weeks earlier Mr. Cardwell had given Malik's class an assignment: Describe an occurrence of force and motion in everyday terms. The assignment was due Thursday. Malik had not begun.

Because Malik missed last week's classes due to the chicken pox, he didn't have a clue as to what force and motion were.

Dashing home from school, Malik immediately sat down to plan his attack. Distracted by his hunger, he sauntered off to a bin in the pantry, grabbed a half-dozen walnuts, and cracked them open with a nutcracker. *Ouch!* Malik accidentally squeezed his pinky finger in the machine. Pain rushed through his hand and arm.

Malik dropped the walnuts just as he heard his dad returning from work. His dad reminded Malik of his promise to tear down the old tree fort. The fort was a dilapidated structure of rusty nails, rotting wood, and mangled rope sitting on three branches overhanging the family's driveway.

Holding a crowbar in his hand, Malik gingerly climbed an extension ladder to gain access to the fort. He pried out nail after nail, dropping hunks of rotting fort to the pavement below. *I sure love destroying stuff,* he thought to himself.

Just then, Malik pried out a spike with a bit too much vigor. The nail shot out of the wood. The crowbar tip snapped back, catching Malik across the corner of his forehead.

Ten minutes later, with the flow of blood from his head stopped, his dad felt reassured that x-rays were not needed. Malik staggered back outside, broom in hand, to clean up the debris on the driveway. Malik was tired and angry. His pinky throbbed and his head was spinning. He had no time for this! Shouldn't school come first? With righteous indignation, Malik took a mighty swipe and...crack!...the broom fractured the radius bone of his left arm.

The following afternoon, each student shared his or her report for science. When Malik's turn came, he stood up. No paper in hand—he was in the emergency room half the night—Malik detailed his sorry excuse. He spoke clearly, dramatically, and even emotionally. He described the nutcracker, the crowbar, and the broom. Then, looking down at his wristwatch, which read 2:13, Malik muttered, "Two-one-three."

"Exactly!" beamed Mr. Cardwell, who was perched on his desk. "Using everyday terms, you have just described force and motion with simple machine levers 2, 1, and 3. Class, please join me in honoring this budding scientist."

0-7424-1956-8 *Complete Library Skills*

The Budding Scientist (cont.)

▶ **Use the story on page 86 to fill in the web.**

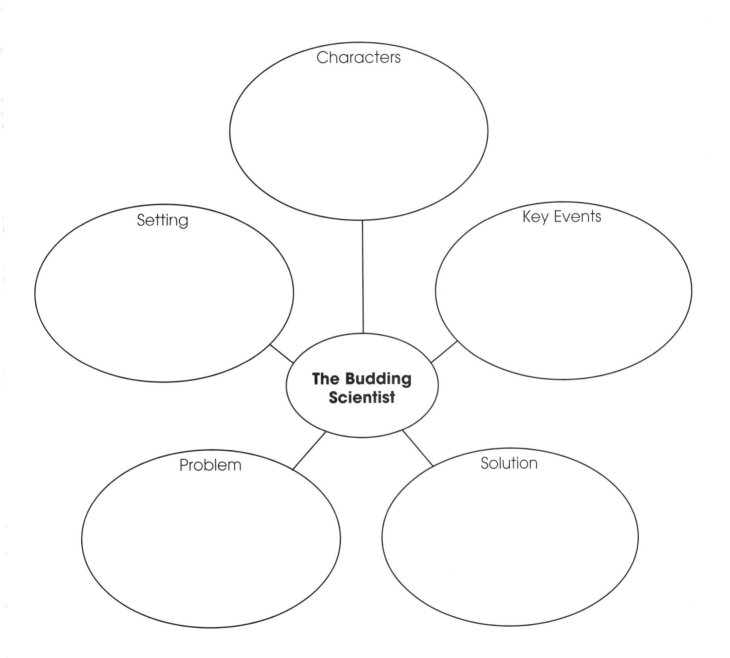

Characters

Setting

Key Events

The Budding Scientist

Problem

Solution

Evaluating Fact and Opinion

When you collect research facts, you should know if you have collected facts or opinions. A *fact* is a statement that is accurate. It has truth. It can be checked as being true. The following is a fact.

> *Baseball is played on a diamond-shaped field.*

An *opinion* is a belief. It is what someone thinks or believes. It may or may not be true. The following is an opinion.

> *Babe Ruth was the best baseball player ever.*

A fact can be supported by other facts. There are certain words that may signal to you that you have collected an opinion. Words such as *believe, feel, think, better,* or *even more* may be a signal that you have an opinion, not a fact.

Let's say that you collect two research statements. The first: *Scientists believe more money should be spent studying space.* The second: *Scientists have been studying problems in space.* Which is fact? Which is opinion? The first is an opinion. Notice the words *believe* and *more* are used. The second statement is a fact. It can be supported by other facts.

1. Write two facts about space.

_____

_____

_____

_____

2. Write two opinions about space.

_____

_____

_____

_____

Is It Fact or Opinion?

Read each statement. Your research may be fact or opinion. If the statement is a fact write *F*. If the statement is an opinion, write *O*.

1. There are many scientists studying the universe. _____

2. We need more scientists than we need other workers. _____

3. We are studying our environment to learn better ways of living. _____

4. I feel animals are an important part of our environment. _____

5. I feel it is healthier to eat vegetables than meat. _____

6. Nutritionists believe that we do not know enough about vitamins. _____

7. The more vitamins you take, the better your health will be. _____

8. Scientists are studying the effects of vitamins. _____

9. I believe the space program is good. _____

10. Scientists are studying the space program. _____

11. History can always be studied. _____

12. It is better to study early history than recent history. _____

13. You should always study something new. _____

14. Learning is growing. _____

15. China is the most populous country. _____

Truth or Lies?

➤ **Read each statement. Your research may be fact or opinion. If the statement is a fact, write *F*. If it is an opinion, write *O*.**

1. I think students should study what they like to learn. _____

2. School presents many subjects for students to study. _____

3. Television is better for young people than other types of entertainment. _____

4. Television offers many different kinds of programs. _____

5. I believe homework helps make students smarter. _____

6. I think we need to learn better ways of eating. _____

7. Scientists say too many fats in a diet are unhealthy. _____

8. Brown eggs are not better than white eggs. _____

9. I believe white eggs are better. _____

10. The space program supports many people. _____

11. The space program is better than it was before. _____

12. We have many scientists in the United States. _____

13. Studying helps improve your learning. _____

14. Homework helps you learn. _____

15. There are many automobiles in the United States. _____

Meaning Mastery

➤ **Use a dictionary to look up the definition of each underlined word. Write the meaning that best fits the context clues in the sentence.**

1. Colorful <u>murals</u> decorate the hallways of the building.

_____

2. The father <u>cradled</u> the baby in his arms.

_____

3. The president met with his <u>cabinet</u> early today.

_____

4. When Anna fell off her bike, she had to wear a <u>dressing</u> on her arm for a week.

_____

5. My brother tried to scare us by <u>disguising</u> his voice.

_____

6. The captain managed to <u>navigate</u> his ship safely through the storm.

_____

7. His <u>sentimental</u> sister cried at the wedding.

_____

8. Ernie was a <u>candidate</u> for class president.

_____

➤ **Choose five underlined words from above and complete the chart below.**

Word	Guide Words	Syllables	Phonetic Spelling

Name _____ Date _____

Word Clues in Context

➤ **Read each of the following sentences. Find the meaning of each underlined word and place the letter of the answer in the blank.**

_____ **1.** The knife was not very sharp, so I had to <u>hack</u> the wood.

_____ **2.** He is bringing home <u>haddock</u> from the sea.

_____ **3.** Our teacher said never to <u>holler</u> in class.

_____ **4.** I sometimes greet my friends with, "<u>Howdy!</u>"

_____ **5.** To control yourself is better than to <u>huff.</u>

_____ **6.** My <u>hound</u> and I like to chase rabbits together.

_____ **7.** Your <u>horrible</u> words made me cry.

_____ **8.** We went to the forest to cut firewood with our <u>hatchet.</u>

_____ **9.** On my plate were a sandwich and a slice of <u>honeydew.</u>

_____ **10.** He keeps a <u>hoard</u> of candy in the back of this closet.

a. to become angry

b. to cut roughly

c. terrible

d. type of fish

e. kind of melon

 f. hidden supply

g. hello

h. type of dog

 i. ax

 j. to shout

➤ **Each of the sentences above has a clue word or words that helped you figure out the meaning of the underlined word. Place each word, the meaning, and the clue in the chart.**

Word	Meaning	Clue(s)

Name _____   Date _____

New Word Bank

➤ **Write down new words you learn at the library.**

New Word	**Definition**
1. _____	_____
2. _____	_____
3. _____	_____
4. _____	_____
5. _____	_____
6. _____	_____
7. _____	_____
8. _____	_____
9. _____	_____
10. _____	_____

Summarizing

Read the three paragraphs below. Circle the best summary for each article.

Charles De Gaulle became a brigadier general early in the Second World War. When the German army advanced and France fell to them, he escaped to London. There he formed a French national committee in exile. With this group he was able to organize the French resistance. Together with other exiled Frenchmen, De Gaulle joined the British to conquer Syria.

1. Which of these sentences best summarizes the article above?

    a. Charles De Gaulle was known for his stubborn determination.
    b. Charles De Gaulle was a French general and leader during World War II.
    c. During World War I Charles De Gaulle was wounded three times and taken prisoner by the Germans.

Erwin Rommel led the Seventh Tank Division as the German forces dashed across the French countryside on their way to the English Channel. Because his moves were so brilliant as commander of the Afrika Korps in North Africa, his friends and enemies called him the Desert Fox. Knowing that the Allied forces would likely attack along the English Channel, the Germans made Rommel responsible for the German defense of Northern France in 1944. After the invasion, Rommel was accused by other German officers of participation in the attempted assassination of Adolf Hitler. In response, Erwin Rommel killed himself.

2. Which of these sentences best summarizes the article above?

    a. Rommel escaped North Africa in 1943 shortly before the Afrika Korps's defeat.
    b. Rommel was a part of the assassination plot against Adolf Hitler.
    c. Erwin Rommel was a famous German soldier who, despite his great military accomplishments, was accused of plotting Hitler's assassination.

Bernard Montgomery was appointed commander of the British Eighth Army in Africa. Although the German army had earlier success there, "Monty" began the offensive at Al 'Alamayn in Egypt, which successfully forced the German and Italian soldiers out. When General Eisenhower became supreme commander of the Allied forces, Montgomery served as the chief of the British forces. In August of 1944, he was promoted to field marshal of British and Canadian troops.

3. Which of these sentences best summarizes the article above?

    a. Bernard Montgomery served his country in its war against Germany and Italy during the Second World War.
    b. General Montgomery was an ardent supporter of General Eisenhower.
    c. Bernard Montgomery was responsible for ridding North Africa of the German troops.

Name _____ Date _____

Puppy Love

➤ **Read the poem below. Answer the questions using complete sentences.**

My owner is the very best,
She pets and plays and all the rest.
I get the best food in my dish,
She's kinder than I'd ever wish.
I'd never put her to the test.

She loves me true, all of the time.
Even with coat covered in grime.
Of course, there are times that she scolds,
But I'm never left out in the cold.
Her love knows no reason or rhyme.

Even as we both grow up
And I'm no longer just a pup,
She hugs and plays and talks to me.
I know two friends we'll always be,
Even when we're both grown up.

I. Summarize the message of this poem. _____

_____

_____

_____

_____

2. Name four things the dog loves about its life. _____

_____

_____

3. What word is a synonym for *dirt*? _____

4. What does "knows no reason or rhyme" mean? _____

_____

_____

_____

_____

Name _____   Date _____

I Like Ike

➤ **Len was given the assignment of researching and writing a brief report about Dwight D. Eisenhower's military career. Read his report and answer the questions on page 97.**

Dwight David Eisenhower, whose real name was David Dwight Eisenhower, was born in Texas, in 1890. Besides being the President of the United States of America, Eisenhower had a brilliant military career. His more than thirty years of military discipline, leadership, and responsibility prepared him for his two terms as president. Called "Ike" by people throughout the world, he was well respected by citizens and world leaders.

Although Eisenhower's family practiced pacifism, he was encouraged by friends to attend the military academy at West Point, where he received a higher education and military training. After graduation in 1915, he began his military career in earnest, quickly going from second lieutenant to first lieutenant in the United States Army. He was on the staff of such great leaders as Brigadier General Fox Conner and General Douglas MacArthur. While serving as MacArthur's aide in the Philippines, he planned the Philippine military defense and helped in organizing a military academy for their newly-formed independent country.

When World War II began, and the United States began to feel it might become involved in that European battle, Eisenhower earned a promotion to brigadier general. By March 1942, after serving in the Army's war plan division, he was promoted to major general, and in June of 1942 was named commanding general of the United States forces in the European Theater of Operations. By 1943, Eisenhower was promoted to four-star general, the highest rank in the Army at that time.

His military abilities so impressed the leaders of the United States, including President Franklin Delano Roosevelt, that Eisenhower was named supreme commander of the Allied Expeditionary Forces in Europe. In this position, he orchestrated the armies and navies of the United States, Great Britain, and other Allied nations, to work together to protect the world from total German invasion. The infamous battle at Normandy, on June 6, 1944, took place under Eisenhower's command.

Even after the German surrender in May of 1945, Eisenhower continued his work for the United States Army. As a five-star general, he was named Army chief of staff in November of 1945— a position he held until his temporary retirement in 1948. With the formation of NATO in 1949, Eisenhower was appointed supreme commander of NATO forces in Europe in 1950. He remained in this position until his Republican nomination for the presidency, a position he held for two full terms.

I Like Ike (cont.)

➤ Answer the questions using the article on page 96.

1. Briefly summarize Eisenhower's military career. Write facts in sequential order, according to the report.

   _____

   _____

   _____

   _____

2. List six different military positions Eisenhower held in the United States Army.

   _____

   _____

   _____

   _____

3. Using the dates given in the essay, make a timeline below showing the progress of Eisenhower's military career.

Using Note Cards to Write Reports

➤ **Below are notes about two types of whales. Divide each set of notes into two subtopics. Arrange the notes on the note cards below. The first one has been started for you.**

Toothed Whales

- average size: 10–30 ft. long
- eat fish, squid, and seals
- largest grow to 60 ft.
- Sperm Whales are largest
- have large teeth to rip up food

Baleen Whales

- eat plankton and small fish
- average size: 50–75 ft. long
- have no teeth
- largest is Blue Whale
- sift tiny fish from water

Topic: Toothed Whales

Subtopic: Size

_____

_____

_____

_____

_____

Topic: Baleen Whales

Subtopic:

_____

_____

_____

_____

_____

Topic:

Subtopic:

_____

_____

_____

_____

_____

Topic:

Subtopic:

_____

_____

_____

_____

_____

Using Note Cards to Write Reports (cont.)

Using the facts from your note cards on page 98, write two paragraphs about whales. The opening sentence for each paragraph has been written for you.

Two Types of Whales

There are two main types of whales. Toothed whales obviously have teeth.

_____

_____

_____

_____

_____

_____

Unlike the toothed whales, baleen whales have no teeth.

_____

_____

_____

_____

_____

_____

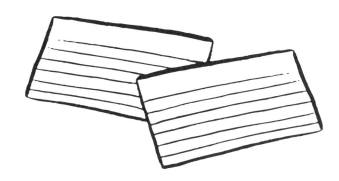

Writing the Report

Your outline and organized note cards become extremely valuable at this point in the project. The hard work you did researching, and your meticulous note taking, will reward you with greater ease in writing. Like other types of writing, the research paper will also contain a beginning, middle, and end.

Beginning

The introductory paragraph will begin with a general statement about your topic. To capture your readers' attention, you may look for a startling statistic, an interesting quotation, or an unusual fact. Sometimes a question may be appropriate. The thesis of your paper, which states the topic and the main points, should also appear in the introduction.

▶ **Write a possible opening sentence for a report on grizzly bears.**

_____

_____

Middle

The body of the paper includes paragraphs that explain each topic. These paragraphs follow the order of the outline and explain the topics included in the thesis statement with reasons, facts, examples, and quotations.

▶ **Write five types of details you might include in the body of a report on grizzly bears.**

_____

_____

End

Your conclusion will restate the important points (main topics) in the paper. Strong conclusions often state what the writer has learned as a result of writing the paper.

▶ **Write a possible concluding sentence for a report on grizzly bears.**

_____

_____

Supporting Your Research Statements

▶ **Read each research statement below. Is it an example, a quotation, a fact or statement, a story, or a definition? Write *example*, *quotation*, *fact*, *story*, or *definition* for each statement.**

1. _____ Let me tell you about my good grades.

2. _____ An ant has three major body parts.

3. _____ "Don't give up the ship!" yelled the captain.

4. _____ "Don't tread on me!" said the colonists.

5. _____ There are over 250 million people in the United States.

6. _____ Let me tell you the strangest thing that ever happened to me.

7. _____ There are two official languages in Canada.

8. _____ There are ten points on the Richter scale.

9. _____ Let me tell you how I first learned to cook.

10. _____ Running can damage your knees.

Backing It Up

➤ **Read each research statement below. Is it an example, a quotation, a fact or statement, a story, or a definition? Write *example*, *quotation*, *fact*, *story*, or *definition* for each statement.**

1. _____ There are one million kites sold in the United States yearly.

2. _____ Kites are known to have been made in early China.

3. _____ Let me tell you how I found my dog.

4. _____ A kite is an object that flies in the sky. It usually is made with paper and string.

5. _____ Many types of kites exist. There are five basic types of kites: the box kite, flat kite, bowed kite, delta kite, and the flexible kite.

6. _____ The flat kite is a kite that always has a tail that is seven times its length.

7. _____ Safety rules for flying kites include: (1) fly in the open, (2) never fly in bad weather, and (3) be certain your kite is well made.

8. _____ Let me tell you about the biggest kite I ever flew.

9. _____ There are over 100,000 kites flown yearly in the United States.

10. _____ "Eureka!" said Benjamin Franklin after he flew his kite.

Making Your Case

▶ **Read each research statement below. Is it an example, a quotation, a fact or statement, a story, or a definition? Write** *example, quotation, fact, story,* **or** *definition* **for each statement.**

1. _____ Ben Franklin said, "A penny saved is a penny earned!"

2. _____ Let me tell you about the funniest day I ever had.

3. _____ Safety rules for swimming include: (1) do not swim alone, (2) do not swim in unsafe waters, and (3) do not swim after eating a heavy meal.

4. _____ There are over one million dolls sold in the United States yearly.

5. _____ "Can you hear me?" asked Alexander Bell.

6. _____ There are about 20,000 types of ants.

7. _____ Reptiles can be found in the mountains.

8. _____ Let me tell you about my camping trip.

9. _____ Let me tell you how to save money when shopping.

Name _____ Date _____

Checklist for Report Writing

➤ **Before you start writing your final report you should know exactly what is expected of you. If your teacher has not told you already, be sure to find out the following:**

Do I need a cover for my report?   YES   NO

Do I need visuals, such as maps, time lines, or pictures?   YES   NO

Should I number the pages?   YES   NO

How long should the report be?   _____ pages

Should I use a pencil, pen, or have it typed?   (circle one)

Should I double space (skip a line) or use every line?   (circle one)

Should I use just one side of my paper or both sides?   (circle one)

Where should my name go?_____

Due Date: _____

Proofing Your Report

Before you turn in your completed report, you need to go over your work to make sure no mistakes crept in as you were writing your final draft.

First, go to a private spot and read your report out loud to yourself. Quite likely, you will be surprised at how funny a sentence may sound when you hear it read.

Second, use the small proofing checklist below to make sure that you have caught all the mechanical mistakes that you may have missed before. These are mistakes having to do with punctuation, grammar, and spelling.

Lastly, give your report to a parent or a friend to read. Ask the person for feedback—is there anything that seems hard to understand, that is illogical, or is out of order? Sometimes when you've been working very hard on a written report it's hard to stand back and look at it critically. It's good to find someone whom you can trust to read the paper and give you honest last-minute advice if needed.

☐ Each sentence begins with a capital letter.

☐ Each sentence ends with a period, question mark, or exclamation point.

☐ All direct quotations are enclosed with quotation marks.

☐ I have checked the spelling of all words I am unsure of.

☐ I have checked for missing words in sentences.

☐ My name is on the report.

 0-7424-1956-8 *Complete Library Skills*

Editing Form

Give your report and this form to a classmate. Ask him or her to read through your report. Then tell this person to put a check mark in a box next to each question. The editor should be sure to provide you with specific comments that will help you improve your paper. Use this form yourself to check your work before turning it in.

Editor's Name _____ Date_____

Report Title _____

	Yes	No	Why?
1. Is the writing interesting?			
2. Are the topic and purpose clear?			
3. Is the introduction strong?			
4. Is the writing colorful?			
5. Does the order make sense?			
6. Are the nouns specific?			
7. Does each sentence begin with a capital letter?			
8. Are the verbs vivid yet accurate?			
9. Is all ending punctuation correct?			
10. Does the title fit the piece?			
11. Did the author use enough different sources?			
12. Does the writing hold your attention?			
13. Is the writing smooth?			
14. Have the paragraphs been indented?			
15. Is there enough information?			
16. Does the paper stick to the topic?			

Writing Foot Notes

Book Footnote

Writing footnotes is simple. Always write the author's name first, then write the name of the book and the page on which you found the information.

Let's say you found a fact about boats in a book called, *Story of Boats* written by T. H. Sail. This is how you would write the footnote.

> T. H. Sail, *The Story of Boats,* p. 10.

Now write a book footnote. You found facts about goldfish on page 26 of *Raising Goldfish* by Ron Gilt.

Magazine Footnote

When you write a footnote for a magazine, always keep in mind that the title of the magazine is included. The author's name is written first. Then write the title of the article in quotes. Italicize the name of the magazine. Always include the date of the magazine. And lastly, write the page number of the first page of the magazine article.

Let's say that you found an article called "How to Fly a Kite" in *Hobby Digest* (April 17, 2000) on page 17. The article was written by John Rogers.

> Rogers, John. "How to Fly a Kite," *Hobby Digest,* April 17, 2000, 17.

Now write a magazine footnote. You found goalie tips on page 10 of the August, 2000 issue of *Hockey Monthly*. Patrick Roy wrote the article titled "The Butterfly Technique."

Encyclopedia Footnote

Writing the footnote for an encyclopedia is simple. First, write the name of the encyclopedia article you are using. Write the name in quotes. Next, write the title of the encyclopedia. The title is italicized. A comma follows, then the year that the encyclopedia was published. It is important to write the year (edition) of the encyclopedia that you are using. Remember, an article about a particular topic may be in the 1996 edition but not in the 2000 edition.

Let's say that you found your information about Paul Revere in an article called "Paul Revere" in the *Encyclopedia of History*. The edition is 1999.

> "Paul Revere," *Encyclopedia of History,* 1999.

Now write an encyclopedia footnote. You found information about greyhounds in an article called "Greyhound" in the 1996 edition of the *Encyclopedia of Canines*.

Book Foot Notes

➡️ **Read the information below. Rewrite each in correct footnote form on the line.**

1. You found your fact on page 13 of *How to Cook* written by Peter Baker.

_____

2. You found your fact on page 58 of *The Key* written by Peter Stick.

_____

3. You found your fact on page 17 of *Science Experiments* written by J. Space.

_____

4. You found your fact on page 42 of *History of the Comics* written by R. Cartoon.

_____

5. You found your fact on page 9 of *Planets* written by Peter Ring.

_____

6. You found your fact on page 7 of *Flowers* written by J. Bloom.

_____

7. You found your fact on page 13 of *Racing* by C. Speck.

_____

Magazine Foot Notes

Read the following information. Rewrite each in correct footnote form on the line.

1. You found your fact on page 13 of "Reptiles: Their Stories" in *Science Digest* (Apr. 17, 1999). It was written by Peter Tail.

_____

2. You found your fact on page 4 of "Snakes" in *Science Digest* (May 13, 1997).

_____

3. You found your fact on page 9 of "Birds" in *Bird Magazine* (Jun. 17, 1999). It was written by Roger Feather.

_____

4. You found your fact on page 21 of "Stars" in *Science World* (Oct. 11, 2000). It was written by James Space.

_____

5. You found your fact on page 47 in "Meteors" in *Science World* (Oct. 11, 2000). It was written by T. Bowser.

_____

6. You found your fact on page 12 in "How to Train Your Puppy" in *Dog Digest* (Apr. 19, 2002) by Peter Collar.

_____

7. You found your fact on page 36 in "Weather and You" in *Science Times* (Apr. 20, 2001) by James Forecast.

_____

Encyclopedia Foot Notes

➡ **Read the information below. Rewrite each in correct footnote form on the line.**

1. Your information is on page 13 of *Encyclopedia of Science* (1999) in an article called "Insects."

_____

2. Your information is on page 39 of *Encyclopedia of Animals* (1997) in an article called "Birds of the World."

_____

3. Your information is on page 57 of *Encyclopedia of Transportation* (2000) in an article called "Sports and Safety Rules."

_____

4. Your information is on page 7 of *Encyclopedia of Wild Animals* (1997) in an article called "Penguins."

_____

5. Your information is on page 70 of *Encyclopedia of Animals* (1999) in an article called "Zebras."

_____

6. Your fact is in the 2000 *Encyclopedia of Transportation* in an article called "Boats and Races."

_____

7. Your fact is in the 2000 *Encyclopedia of Machinery* in an article called "Machines for the New Millenium."

_____

8. Your fact is in the 1999 *Encyclopedia of Science* in an article called "Sandstorms and Weather."

_____

9. Your fact is in the 2000 *Encyclopedia of Cooking* in an article called "Japanese Cooking."

_____

10. Your fact is in the 2001 *Encyclopedia of Games* in an article called "Learning Chess."

_____

Name _____   Date _____

Writing a Bibliography

Book Bibliography

A bibliography is an alphabetized list of resources used in a report. It is alphabetized by the writers' last names. Let's say you found some of the information for your report on sailboats in the book *The Story of Boats*. It was written by T. H. Sail in Boatweave, New Jersey, in 1989 and published by Wave Press Publishers. Your bibliography entry would look like this:

Sail, T. H. *The Story of Boats*. Boatweave, New Jersey: Wave Press, 1989.

➤ **Now write a book entry. You used *A History of Comic Illustration* by Mary Martin. It was published in Cheektowaga, NY in 2000 by Funnyman Press.**

_____

Magazine Bibliography

First write the author's name (last name first). Then write the name of the article in quotes. Write the name of the magazine in italics. Be certain to write its date. This helps readers to locate the magazine more quickly. Finally, include the page numbers on which the article is found. Let's say that you found information about training parakeets in *Pet Magazine* in an article written by William Rogers called, "How to Train Your Parakeet" (Apr. 7, 1999) on pages 85–87. Your bibliography entry would look like this:

Rogers, William. "How to Train Your Parakeet." *Pet Magazine* (April 7, 1999), 85–87.

Now write a magazine entry. Interesting information on catfish can be found in the May 1, 2003 issue of *Aquarium Times*. The article, by S. Whisker, is titled "How to Keep Your Catfish Going" and is on pages 30–33.

_____

Encyclopedia Bibliography

The title of the encyclopedia article comes first in quotes. The title of the encyclopedia follows and then the year or edition. After the date comes the volume number and the pages the article is found on. Let's say that you found information about pirates in the *Encyclopedia of History* (2001) in an article called "Pirates." Your bibliography entry would look like this:

"Pirates." *Encyclopedia of History*. 2001. Volume 18, pp. 188–191.

Now write an encyclopedia entry. Go to the 1996 edition of the *Earth Book Encyclopedia*, Volume 1, for great facts about mammals. The article is titled "Animals" and is on pages 56–66.

_____

Citing Books

Read the information about books below. Then write each in the correct bibliography form.

1. *Your Aquarium* was published in Deepsea, New Jersey in 1985. It was written by Peter Fish and published by Scale Press.

_____

2. *All About Ants* was published by Hill Press in Anthill, Ohio in 1987. It was written by John Picnic.

_____

3. *The History of Space* was published by Star Press in Startown, New Jersey in 1989. It was written by Peter Spacecraft.

_____

4. *Sports,* by John Game, was published in 1997 by Goal Press in Endtown, New York.

_____

5. *The History of Cartoons,* by Roger Funny, was published by Color Press in Flower, New York in 1999.

_____

6. *Rocks and Minerals,* by Roger Stone, was published by Stone Press in Boulder, Colorado in 1989.

_____

7. *Toys in History,* by C. R. Doll, was published in Dollhouse, New York by Ragtime Press in 1989.

_____

8. *Boats in History,* by Peter Sail, was published in Wave, New York by Ocean Press in 1986.

_____

Citing Books (cont.)

Read the information about books below. Then write each in correct bibliography form.

1. *Baseball,* by Roger Base, was written in 1989 and published by Diamond Press in Diamond, New York.

_____

2. *Sports Legends,* by Richard Base, was written in 1985 and published by Legend Press in Diamond, New York.

_____

3. *Starfish,* by Linda Sea, was published in 1989 by Wave Press in Oceanside, New Jersey.

_____

4. *Plants and You,* by Lynn Budd, was published in 1985 by Leaf Press in Stem, New York.

_____

5. *Cars,* by Roger Wheel, was published by Horn Press in Station, New York in 1993.

_____

6. *Raising Your Puppy,* by C. W. Biscuit, was published by Bow Wow Press in Spaniel, New York in 1989.

_____

7. *Spacecraft,* by Peter Tripp, was published by Ship Press in Travel, New York in 1986.

_____

Citing Magazines

➧ **Read the information about magazines below. Then write each in correct bibliography form.**

1. Your facts are from an article called "Snakes" by C. Slink in *Science Digest* (Jun. 17, 1999) on page 75.

_____

2. Your facts are from an article called "Bicycle and Safety" by John Ride in *Hobby Digest* (Jun. 21, 2002) on page 65.

_____

3. Your facts are from an article titled "Learning to Paint" by C. W. Brush in *Arts and Crafts* (Jun. 19, 2002) on page 47.

_____

4. Your facts are from "Rabbits and Gerbils" in *Pet Digest* (Jul. 13, 2003) on page 63, by Roger Pet.

_____

5. Your facts are from "Cars" in *Car Digest* (Aug. 12, 2000) on page 48, by Peter Wheel.

_____

6. Your facts are from "The Latest Fashion Trends" in *Teen Digest* (Sept. 2002) on page 99, by R. Dress.

_____

7. Your facts are from "Eye Shadow and You" in *Teen Digest* (Sept. 2002) on page 33, by R. Lash.

_____

Name _____ Date _____

Citing Encyclopedias

▶ **Read the information about encyclopedias below. Then write each in correct bibliography form.**

1. Your facts are from an article called "Washington" in the *Encyclopedia of American History* (1997) on page 11.

_____

2. Your facts are from an article called "Starting Your Rock Collection" in the *Encyclopedia of Science* (1999) on page 10.

_____

3. Your facts are from an article called "The Jungle" in the *Encyclopedia of Science* (2002) on page 31.

_____

4. Your facts are from an article called "The Movies" in the *Encyclopedia of Science* (2002) on page 39.

_____

5. Your facts are from an article called "Space and Stars" in the *Encyclopedia of Science* (2002) on page 59.

_____

6. Your facts are from "Training Your Parakeet" in the *Encyclopedia of Pets* (1996) on page 49.

_____

7. Your facts are from "History of Cartoons" in the *Encyclopedia of Arts* (1999) on page 307.

_____

Citing Database Sources

When using articles or periodicals from an electronic database, you will need to cite these materials in footnotes and in a bibliography. Look at the example below for a bibliography and a footnote. These are done in MLA (Modern Language Association) style.

Bibliography

Weeks, Hillary. "Learning About Computer Research." *Daily News,* 30 Nov., 1997. CD NewsBank from NewsBank, Inc.

Footnote

Hillary Weeks. "Learning About Computer Research." *Daily News,* 30 Nov., 1997: CD NewsBank from NewsBank, Inc.

➡ **Now work backward. Write the following information from the CD-ROM database that was used above.**

1. Author _____

2. Title _____

3. Newspaper title _____

4. Date _____

5. Database _____

Database Citation

Pretend you used information from an article in the **CD NewBank** database titled **"How to Invest Your Allowance" by C. W. Dollar on December 4, 1994,** in the newspaper *Your Money*. **List below the specific article information requested. Then write bibliography and footnote citations for the article on the lines at the bottom of the page, using MLA style.**

1. Author _____

2. Title _____

3. Newspaper title _____

4. Date _____

5. Database _____

Bibliography

_____

_____

_____

_____

_____

Footnote

_____

_____

_____

_____

_____

Citing Online Sources

Just as you must give credit to the authors of print materials, you need to also cite many sources you find on the Internet. Since following the path you took to get to a source can be tricky, follow the guidelines below as closely as you can. It's important to remember that stable, well-organized Web sites will probably be easier to cite. You should always include the title of the online article, the author, and the Web address (URL). If there is no author, write the name of the main Web site or the company that owns the copyright. Look at the example below.

You find details about great white sharks, and you write this citation:

Short, Renae. "The Great White Shark." 21 March, 2001
http://www.umich.edu/science/vertebrates/gwshark.html

1. What is the title of the page on this Web site?

_____

2. Who wrote this material?

_____

3. On what date was the material first written or posted?

_____

4. Put the following elements in order by writing *1, 2, 3,* and *4.*

_____ Web address

_____ author

_____ page or article title

_____ publication date

Giving Them Credit

➤ **Look at the Web page below. Write a bibliography citation for this page.**

_____

http://www.geography.com/timezones.html

TIME ZONES

When it is daytime in the United States, is it daytime all around the world?

No. When it is daytime in the United States, the United States is facing the sun. Days and nights come about as Earth rotates on its axis. When it is daytime in the United States it is nighttime in Asia, for example, because Asia is on the side of Earth facing away from the sun.

Even in the United States, the time is not the same in every state. The United States is divided into different time zones. The time can differ by as much as a few hours from state to state. And times in time zones can change with daylight savings time.

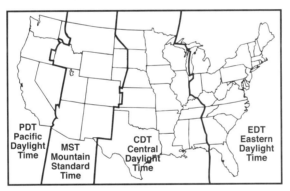

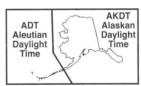

copyright © Geography Nation, Inc. June 1, 1999.

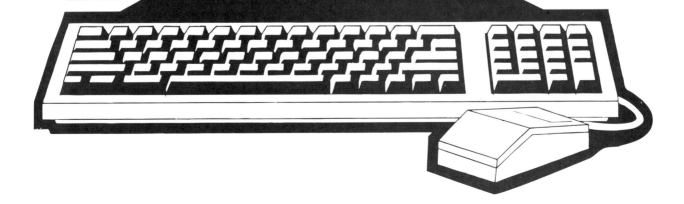

Glossary

almanac—yearly publication with statistics on various events

appendix—any materials the author wishes to add to the body of the book such as tables or lists of information; it is found at the back of the book.

atlas—a bound collection of maps

author card—catalog card that is alphabetized by author's last name

author search—to search the online library catalog by author

autobiography—a true story about a person's life written by that person

biographical encyclopedia—a dictionary that contains information pertaining to the facts and events of a person's life

bibliography—an alphabetized list of materials that gives the following information: author's name; source title, place, and date of publication; name of publisher; and page numbers of magazine or encyclopedia article

biography—a true story of a person's life written by someone other than that person

body of book—the main part of the book

book index—an alphabetized list of topics or subjects that can be found in a book

browser—a computer application that allows you to search a database, such as a library catalog or the World Wide Web

browser station—area in a library where computers used to search the library catalog are located

Caldecott Medal—an annual award for the best picture book published in the previous year

call number—a number/letter combination associated with every piece of library material that shows its location in the library and often its topic

card catalog—a collection of reference cards arranged alphabetically by author, title, and subject

CD-ROM—computer disk that contains searchable databases or games

CD-ROM database—a searchable group of articles contained on a CD-ROM

character—an animal, a person, or a nonhuman object in a story, play, poem, or short story

cite—to give credit to an individual or organization

climax—the highest point of tension in a story

Glossary

copyright date—the date that the work was first published or republished

copyright page—found at the front of a book; it gives the book's title, author, publisher, place of publication, and copyright date.

conclusion—the end of a story, play, or short story

decimal—a part of a number represented using numbers and a point (example: 796.10)

Dewey Decimal Classification®—system that arranges nonfiction books according to ten major divisions

dialogue—conversations in a play, novel, or short story

encyclopedia—a reference work that contains articles on a variety of subjects and is organized alphabetically

encyclopedia cross reference—found at the end of an article in an encyclopedia; it suggests other subjects to check under for additional information.

encyclopedia guidewords—found at the top of the page; topics are found alphabetically between these words used as guides.

encyclopedia index—alphabetized list of subjects found in an encyclopedia

encyclopedia key words—words under which you would most likely find information you seek

encyclopedia "see also" references—found at the end of an article; these are additional subjects where information can be found.

entry—information given under a word in a reference book; entries are in alphabetical order.

fable—short, simple story that usually contains a moral or lesson

fairy tale—simple story that has a hero, a problem, and a happy ending

falling action—story events that lead to the end

fantasy—story that creates an imaginary world

fiction—story that does not tell actual events

footnote—a note of reference or explanation that is placed at the bottom of a report page giving the reader specific information about where to find the data in the report

free write—to write down everything one knows about a topic without worrying about form, grammar, or facts; used as a brainstorming tool

Glossary

geographical dictionary—a dictionary that includes geographic information, including spelling of places around the world

globe—a spherical, three-dimensional representation/map of Earth

glossary—a mini-dictionary of terms used in a book; it is usually found at the back of a book

guide letters—letters placed on the outside of card catalog drawers that tell what cards are in the drawer

index—an alphabetized list of topics or subjects that can be found in a book

Internet—the worldwide interconnected network of computers

historical fiction—a make-believe story about a real person or a real time that existed in the past

humor—a funny story

keyword search—to search the online library catalog by key words associated with a topic

mystery—a piece of fiction writing dealing with the solution of a mysterious crime

myth—story that tells the trials and successes of a hero; it is usually a story created by people to explain something in life, for example why it rains or snows.

Newbery Medal—an annual award for the best contribution to children's literature in the previous year

nonfiction—story that retells actual events

outline—a summary of a written work, usually using headings and subheadings

play—story told by characters in dialogue

poetry—a verse or rhyme

point of view—the author's attitude and opinions about a subject

preface—an explanation found at the beginning of a book that explains the ideas of the author, such as why he or she wrote the book

research—to investigate a topic thoroughly

romance—a work of fiction about a love story

science fiction—fantasy story usually dealing with another time, another place, and often other beings; definite rules do exist within the framework of this created world.

search engine—a tool used to find Web sites on the World Wide Web

Glossary

shelf labels—gives a range for what is located on a library shelf

skim—to scan an article to understand the main idea without reading all of the words

subject card—catalog card that is alphabetized by the subject

subject search—to search the online library catalog by subject heading

table of contents—listing of contents found at the beginning of a book

tall tale—a story so exaggerated it could not be true

theme—major idea of a story, play, or other work

thesaurus—a resource book that contains words and their synonyms and often their antonyms

title card—catalog card that is alphabetized by the title of the book

title search—to search the online library catalog by title

tone—the feeling of the written word, story, play, or poem

vertical file—a collection of items too small to be placed on library shelves; these may include pamphlets, newspaper clippings, pictures, and posters.

Web site—a location on the World Wide Web that contains information about a particular topic, person, or company

World Wide Web—an interconnection of computers worldwide that is searchable through the use of a search engine

0-7424-1956-8 *Complete Library Skills*

Answer Key

For pages in which answers will vary, no answer key is provided.

What's in the Library? 5
1. e
2. f
3. g
4. h
5. i
6. j
7. a
8. c
9. b
10. d
11–12. Answers will vary.

Understanding the Decimal in the System 8
handball—796.31
volleyball—796.32

It's Got Class 9
1. 000–099 General Reference
2. 300–399 Social Science
3. 300–399 Social Science
4. 800–899 Literature
5. 900–999 History
6. 300–399 Social Science
7. 200–299 Religion
8. 000–099 General Reference
9. 500–599 Science
10. 900–999 History
11. 300–399 Social Science
12. 800–899 Literature
13. 500–599 Science
14. 800–899 Literature
15. 700–799 Fine Arts

Research Situations 10
1. 570
2. 790
3. 580
4. 790
5. 970
6. 750
7. 790
8. 640
9. 570
10. 520

What Subject Division? 11
1. 550
2. 520
3. 570
4. 570
5. 570
6. 640
7. 790
8. 900
9. 740
10. 920
11. 440
12. 790
13. 970
14. 970
15. 570

16. 930
17. 790
18. 460
19. 790
20. 970

What Division Do You Need? 12
1. 790; recreational arts
2. 920; general biography
3. 390; customs, etiquette, folklore
4. 390; customs, etiquette, folklore
5. 460; Spanish & Portuguese languages
6. 640; home economics & family living
7. 970; general history of North America
8. 910; general geography & travel
9. 250; local church and religious orders
10. 570; life sciences

Putting Call Numbers in Order 13
1. 4, 2, 3, 1, 5
2. 5, 4, 2, 1, 3
3. 2, 1, 4, 3, 5
4. 3, 1, 2, 5, 4
5. 2, 1, 4, 3, 5
6. 2, 3, 1, 5, 4

Using the Card Catalog 14
New Jersey, Roger State,
state history

Comparing Cards 15
1. 567 So and 567 Sy
2. *The Planets*
3. Galaxy Press and Milky Way Press
4. 567 So
5. *Stars, Galaxies, and the Planets*
6. planets
7. Jason Solar
8. Peter System
9. Startown, NY
10. New York

What Card Catalog Do You Need? 16
1. author or title
2. subject
3. subject
4. subject
5. author or title
6. subject
7. author or title
8. subject
9. title
10. author or title

Name That Card 17
1. title
2. subject
3. author
4. title
5. author
6. subject
7. title
8. author
9. subject
10. title
11. subject
12. title
13. author
14. title
15. subject

Title Search 19
1. He typed the word *the*.
2. It doesn't matter if you use capital letters.
3. He should choose record number 2.
4. He should expect to find either cassette tapes or a CD.

Author Search 20
1. 2002
2. 796.72 Fas
3. 96 pages
4. 500 Press; Indiana
5. No; this book only talks about race car safety.

Subject Search 21
1. 2
2. 1
3. 1; You don't want to trap the squirrels, just keep them away from the bird feeder.

Keyword Search 22
1. keyword search
2. It helped narrow the topic of soccer.
3. He would have gotten titles on soccer but not on training.
4. If an online catalog does not have a subject heading for the topic you are interested in, a keyword search would be more helpful.

How to Read the Online Card Catalog 23–24
1. home economics & family living
2. Literature; American Literature in English
3. yes; it is available.
4. You would do an author search with this author's name.

Let's Get Cooking **25**
1. *Complete Microwave Cookbook*
2. *African Cooking*
3. *Japanese Cooking*
4. *Vegetarian Cooking Around the World*
5. 641.5 KER; Kerr, Graham; *A Low Fat, Heart Healthy Cookbook;* G. P. Putnam's; 1995
6. 2
7. Time-Life
8. *The Complete Diabetic Cookbook; Vegetarian Cooking Around the World; Watching Your Weight Cookbook; A Low Fat, Heart Healthy Cookbook*

Let's Get Cooking **26**
1. 1968 and 1970
2. Coralie Castle
3. *Food in India*
4. 1990
5. China, France, Middle East
6. Ameil—1977 and Barron's—1984
7. Paolo Gomez
8. yes
9. *Food in Italy; Scandinavian Cooking*

Audio Equipment **28**
1. Car stereo update
2. Road music and Signals: pony car
3. Car stereo update
4. Car stereo update
5. Signals: pony car
6. Car stereo update

Audio Equipment **29**
1. Stealth stereo upgrades
2. Road music
3. Stealth stereo upgrades
4. Stealth stereo upgrades
5. All
6. Road music
7. Car stereo update

Genres of Literature **32**
1. mystery
2. nonfiction
3. biography
4. tall tale
5. autobiography
6. fiction
7. poetry
8. science fiction
9. humor
10. historical fiction
11. fable
12. fantasy

Can You Tell a Book by Its Cover? **33**
1. cooking
2. mystery
3. romance
4. myth
5. poetry
6. dictionary
7. atlas
8. East Asian folk tale
9. foreign language
10. song book
11. science fiction
12. American history
13. stars
14. nursery rhymes
15. Ancient Egypt
16. medieval history
17. inventions
18. engine repair
19. sports stars
20. art appreciation
21. thesaurus
22. gardening
23. ESP
24. American dance
25. autobiography

Keywords and Search Terms **39**
pollution, waters, environment

Evaluating Online Sources ....**pages 42–43**
1. b
2. a
3. Answers will vary.

Can You Spy the Best Site? ....**pages 44–45**
1. a
2. c
3. a
4. b
5. a

Choosing CD-ROM Databases **46**
1. 2
2. 2
3. 2
4. 4
5. 2
6. 4
7. 1

Selecting Sample History Databases **47**
1. Atlas of U.S. Presidents
2. African-American History
3. Famous Places
4. Encyclopedia of the American Revolution
5. World History Fact Book
6. Encyclopedia of Native Americans
7. Atlas of U.S. Presidents
8. U.S. History
9. U.S. Geography
10. African-American History

Choosing Topics **49**
1. broad, narrow, good
2. narrow, broad, good
3. good, narrow, broad
4. broad, good, narrow
5. broad, good, narrow
6. broad, good, narrow
7. good, broad, narrow
8. good, narrow, broad

Picking the Best Topic **50**
1. good, narrow, broad
2. narrow, good, broad
3. good, broad, narrow
4. narrow, good, broad
5. narrow, good, broad
6. broad, good, narrow
7. broad, good, narrow

Using a Magazine Guide— Hobbies **54**
1. Baseball Card Collecting
2. Stamps of the World: Building Your Collection
3. Football for Teens
4. All About Chess
5. Painting for Kids and Water Color Painting for Young People
6. Dolls: Making Clothes
7. All About Baseball
8. Coin Collecting
9. Football for Teens
10. Stamp Collecting and Stamps of the World: Building Your Collection

Answer Key

Using a Magazine Guide—Cooking 55
1. Cakes for Special Occasions
2. Cooking and Nutrition
3. Vitamins and Cooking
4. Decorating Cakes
5. Baking for Kids
6. Cakes for Special Occasions
7. Making Dinner
8. Cookies for Holidays
9. Baking for Kids
10. Cooking and Nutrition and Vitamins and Cooking

Termite Book Index 56
1. 129
2. 87
3. 93
4. 29
5. 36
6. 3
7. 87
8. 2
9. 93
10. 17

Toy Book Index 57
1. 89
2. 79
3. 121
4. 167 or 57
5. 183
6. 33
7. 31
8. 31
9. 121
10. 79

Using an Almanac 58
1. 373
2. 372
3. 170, 486
4. 168
5. 169–170
6. 820
7. 868
8. 865
9. 350–359
10. 97

Almanac Review.......................59
1. 153
2. 154
3. 155
4. 156
5. 153
6. 156
7. 156
8. 154
9. 155
10. 155

Using a Biographical Dictionary 60
1. He retired from political life.
2. 1900
3. New York City
4. He took care of his plantation.
5. yes
6. Westmoreland County, VA
7. Culpeper County, VA
8. 1774–1775
9. no
10. Morristown, NJ

Using an Encyclopedia Index 61
1. *Encyclopedia of Travel* S-496
2. no
3. 135
4. 89
5. no
6. sailboats, speedboats
7. *Encyclopedia of Travel* A-91
8. yes
9. yes; *Encyclopedia of Travel* B-367
10. no

Comparing Encyclopedia Indices 62
1. *Encyclopedia of the World,* S-329
2. *Encyclopedia of the World*
3. no
4. no
5. yes; *World* H-565
6. yes; *World* B-401
7. yes; *Knowledge* I-309
8. Arts and Crafts, Drawing, Painting
9. *Encyclopedia of Knowledge,* S-117
10. no

Endangered Species Chart 64
1. Common Name, Scientific Name, Distribution, and Survival Problem
2. balaenoptera musculus
3. habitat destruction and over-hunting
4. India
5. Florida, Mexico, Central and South Caribbean islands, India
6. black-footed ferret
7. black-footed ferret and California condor
8. imperial parrot

Space Probes Chart 65
1. Date Launched, Name, Launched By, and Accomplishments
2. *Luna 9*
3. *Luna 10*
4. Sept. 12, 1970
5. U.S.A.
6. *Ranger 4*
7. *Venera 4*
8. Jupiter

Reading a Time Line 66
1. 1000–1690
2. 1577
3. 1682
4. no
5. 1510–1540
6. 1513
7. Drake and Raleigh
8. 1540–1570 and 1630–1660
9. Marquette, Joliet, and La Salle

Using Time Line Information 67
1. June 1914–November 1918
2. June 1914
3. Russia signs treaty and Germany's final attack
4. Allies
5. August 1914
6. Allies use tanks for the first time
7. April 1917
8. May 1915
9. the war ends

Finding Information in a Table 68
1. Year, Winner, Loser, and Site
2. Pittsburgh Steelers
3. 35-10
4. Baltimore Colts
5. 1970

Tables Are Helpful 69
1. Railroad, Train, From, To, Distance, Time, and Speed
2. miles
3. Amtrak and Via Rail Canada
4. minutes
5. 47 minutes
6. Trenton
7. 85.1 mph
8. Wilmington

A Man Remembered..........pages 84–85
1. one of 17 children; poor; did not get a good education; attended school until age 10; taught himself
2. stamps, $100 bill
3. newspaper, almanac
4. bifocals; wood-burning stove; established an academy of learning; first city hospital

The Budding Scientist ....pages 86–87
Characters: Malik, Dad, Mr. Cardwell
Setting: home, school
Key Events: Malik misses school, squeezes finger, hits head, breaks arm, gives report
Problem: Malik does not complete his report on force and motion.
Solution: By describing his activities, Malik successfully completes his report.

Is It Fact or Opinion? 89
1. F
2. O
3. F
4. O
5. O
6. O
7. O
8. F
9. O
10. F
11. F
12. O
13. O
14. O
15. F

Truth or Lies? 90
1. O
2. F
3. O
4. F
5. O
6. O
7. F
8. O
9. O
10. F
11. O
12. F
13. O
14. O
15. F

Meaning Mastery 91
1. a large painting applied to a wall
2. to hold protectively
3. a group of advisors
4. bandage
5. to obscure
6. steer
7. easily affected by emotions
8. person running for office
Chart will vary.

Word Clues in Context 92
1. b
2. d
3. j
4. g
5. a
6. h
7. c
8. i
9. e
10. f
Chart will vary.

Summarizing 94
1. b
2. c
3. a

Puppy Love 95
1. The owner and puppy both love each other.
2. food, play, mud, not cold. etc.
3. grime
4. Her love is endless.

I Like Ike....................pages 96–97
1. Answers will vary. Possible answer is: Eisenhower begin his military career at West Point. He quickly moved up in rank, impressing his superiors with his abilities. He worked with such famous men as Fox Conner and Douglas MacArthur. Eisenhower was a part of major military situations, including Philippine independence and the battle of Normandy, during World War II.
2. Eisenhower held the positions of second lieutenant, first lieutenant, brigadier general, major general, four-star general, and five-star general.
3. Time line should include the date/years mentioned in the essay.

Using Note Cards to Write Reports 98–99
Toothed Whales
Subtopic: Size
average size: 10–30 ft.
largest: 60 ft.
Sperm Whales are largest.
Subtopic: Food
eat fish, squid, and seals
large teeth rip up food
Baleen Whale
Subtopic: Size
average size: 50–75 ft.
largest: Blue Whale
Subtopic: Food
eat plankton and small fish
have no teeth
sift tiny fish from water

Supporting Your Research Statements 101
1. story
2. fact
3. quotation
4. quotation
5. fact
6. story
7. fact
8. fact
9. story
10. fact

Backing It Up 102
1. fact
2. fact
3. story
4. definition
5. example
6. definition
7. example
8. story
9. fact
10. quotation

Making Your Case 103
1. quotation
2. story
3. example
4. fact
5. quotation
6. fact
7. fact
8. story
9. story

Writing Foot Notes 107
Ron Gilt, *Raising Goldfish*, p. 26.
Roy, Patrick. "The Butterfly Technique," *Hockey Monthly*, August, 2000, 10.
"Greyhound," *Encyclopedia of Canines*, 1996.

Answer Key

Book Foot Notes 108
1. Peter Baker, *How to Cook*, p. 13.
2. Peter Stick, *The Key*, p. 58.
3. J. Space, *Science Experiments*, p. 17.
4. R. Cartoon, *History of the Comics*, p. 42.
5. Peter Ring, *Planets*, p. 9.
6. J. Bloom, *Flowers*, p. 7.
7. C. Speck, *Racing*, p. 13.

Magazine Foot Notes 109
1. Tail, Peter. "Reptiles: Their Stories," *Science Digest*, April 17, 1999, 13.
2. "Snakes," *Science Digest*, May 13, 1997, 4.
3. Feather, Roger. "Birds," *Bird Magazine*, June 17, 1999, 9.
4. Space, James. "Stars," *Science World*, October 11, 2000, 21.
5. Bowser, T. "Meteors," *Science World*, October 11, 2000, 47.
6. Collar, Peter. "How to Train Your Puppy," *Dog Digest*, April 19, 2002, 12.
7. Forecast, James. "Weather and You," *Science Times*, April 20, 2001, 36.

Encyclopedia Foot Notes 110
1. "Insects," *Encyclopedia of Science*, 1999.
2. "Birds of the World," *Encyclopedia of Animals*, 1997.
3. "Sports and Safety Rules," *Encyclopedia of Transportation*, 2000.
4. "Penguins," *Encyclopedia of Wild Animals*, 1997.
5. "Zebras," *Encyclopedia of Animals*, 1999.
6. "Boats and Races," *Encyclopedia of Transportation*, 2000.
7. "Machines for the New Millenium," *Encyclopedia of Machinery*, 2000.
8. "Sandstorms and Weather," *Encyclopedia of Science*, 1999.
9. "Japanese Cooking," *Encyclopedia of Cooking*, 2000.
10. "Learning Chess," *Encyclopedia of Games*, 2001.

Writing a Bibliography 111
Martin, Mary. *A History of Comic Illustration*. Cheektowaga, NY; Funnyman Press, 2000.
Whisker, S. "How to Keep Your Catfish Going." *Aquarium Times* (May 1, 2003), 30–33.
"Animals." *Earth Book Encyclopedia*. 1996. Volume 1, pp. 56–66.

Citing Books 112
1. Fish, Peter. *Your Aquarium*. Deepsea, New Jersey: Scale Press, 1985.
2. Picnic, John. *All About Ants*. Anthill, Ohio: Hill Press, 1987.
3. Spacecraft, Peter. *The History of Space*. Startown, New Jersey: Star Press, 1989.
4. Game, John. *Sports*. Endtown, New York: Goal Press, 1997.
5. Funny, Roger. *The History of Cartoons*. Flower, New York: Color Press, 1999.
6. Stone, Roger. *Rocks and Minerals*. Boulder, Colorado: Stone Press, 1989.
7. Doll, C. R. *Toys in History*. Dollhouse, New York: Ragtime Press, 1989.
8. Sail, Peter. *Boats in History*. Wave, New York: Ocean Press, 1986.

Citing Books 113
1. Base, Roger. *Baseball*. Diamond, New York: Diamond Press, 1989.
2. Base, Richard. *Sports Legends*. Diamond, New York: Legend Press, 1985.
3. Sea, Linda. *Starfish*. Oceanside, New Jersey: Wave Press, 1989.
4. Budd, Lynn. *Plants and You*. Stem, New York: Leaf Press, 1985.
5. Wheel, Roger. *Cars*. Station, New York: Horn Press, 1993.
6. Biscuit, C. W. *Raising Your Puppy*. Spaniel, New York: Bow Wow Press, 1989.
7. Tripp, Peter. *Spacecraft*. Travel, New York: Ship Press, 1986.

Citing Magazines 114
1. Slink, C. "Snakes." *Science Digest* (June 17, 1999), 75.
2. Ride, John. "Bicycle and Safety." *Hobby Digest* (June 21, 2002), 65.
3. Brush, C. W. "Learning to Paint." *Arts and Crafts* (June 19, 2002), 47.
4. Pet, Roger. "Rabbits and Gerbils." *Pet Digest* (July 13, 2003), 63.
5. Wheel, Peter. "Cars." *Car Digest* (August 12, 2000), 48.
6. Dress, R. "The Latest Fashion Trends." *Teen Digest* (Sept. 2002), 99.
7. Lash, R. "Eye Shadow and You." *Teen Digest* (Sept. 2002), 33.

Citing Encyclopedias 115
1. "Washington." *Encyclopedia of American History*. 1997, p. 11.
2. "Starting Your Rock Collection." *Encyclopedia of Science*. 1999, p. 10.
3. "The Jungle." *Encyclopedia of Science*. 2002, p. 31.
4. "The Movies." *Encyclopedia of Science*. 2002, p. 39.
5. "Space and Stars." *Encyclopedia of Science*. 2002, p. 59.
6. "Training Your Parakeet." *Encyclopedia of Pets*. 1996, p. 49.
7. "History of Cartoons." *Encyclopedia of Arts*. 1999, p. 307.

Citing Database Sources 116
1. Hillary Weeks
2. "Learning About Computer Research"
3. *Daily News*
4. Nov. 30, 1997
5. CD NewsBank

Database Citation 117
1. C. W. Dollar
2. "How to Invest Your Allowance"
3. *Your Money*
4. December 4, 1994
5. CD NewsBank
Bibliography:
   Dollar, C. W. "How to Invest Your Allowance." *Your Money*. 4 Dec., 1994. CD NewsBank from NewsBank, Inc.
Footnote:
   C. W. Dollar. "How to Invest Your Allowance." *Your Money*, 4 Dec., 1994: CD NewsBank from NewBank, Inc.

Citing Online Sources 118
1. "The Great White Shark"
2. Renae Short
3. March 21, 2001
4. author, title, date, address

Giving Them Credit 119
Geography Nation, Inc. "Time Zones." 1 June, 1999 <http://www.geography.com/timezones.html>
